CHARACTERS OF FAKENHAM

Compiled by Raymond Monbiot

Published in 2016 by

Raymond Monbiot Books
Eastgate House, Burnham Market
Norfolk PE31 8HH

ISBN 978-0-9542567-4-6

Typesetting:
Raymond Monbiot

Printed by:
Newprint and Design Ltd, Fakenham, Norfolk
Tel . 01328 851578

Cover photos
Front: Denise Pearson and Archy
Inside Front: Gerald and Denise Benbow
Inside Back: Martin and Jennie Turner
Back Cover: Willie Parker

Contents page

Introduction

I had written and published four books about interesting characters in North Norfolk when Brigitte Doughty inspired me to write a fifth - this time based on Fakenham.   There is no shortage of interesting people in and around the town and available space in the book has alone determined the number included in this volume: *The Characters of Fakenham.*
The town stands out from other rural and agricultural settlements in Norfolk because, in addition to its agricultural heritage it has a strong and impressive industrial history.   It took many centuries to get there but it became dominant in gas and printing.   Fakenham is recorded in the Domesday Book published in 1086. Dr Mike Bridges, distinguished academic and historian, describes the population growth thus :

> *"It is on record that the Manor of Fakenham, which had belonged to King Harold, was given by King William to Earl de Warrene, whose family held it until 1377 when it passed to the Duchy of Lancaster, so acquiring the town's full name of Fakenham-Lancaster. Interpreting the Domesday Book record, it is thought between 100 and 150 people lived in Fakenham at the time.   In the census of 1801 the population of the town is given as 1236 and fifty years later it had grown to 2240.   Growth continued up to 1911 when just over 3000 inhabitants were counted.   In the five decades since 1951 the population has increased by around 1000 per decade and at the millennium stood at about 8000 and is now around 9000." (Ref. E. M. Bridges: Fakenham-Lancaster2010).*

Now, in 2016, there is anticipation of rapid growth of up to 1000 new houses and an increase in population of 3500 or so in the north of the town.   The opportunity is presented for new amenities, jobs, restaurants and shops to satisfy the aspirations of new and existing residents, second homers and visitors.   In Holt, Dereham and Burnham Market and to a lesser extent, Fakenham, they take advantage of their leisure to browse and buy goods and services locally, in a way that is impossible in London and other large towns and cities where people lead busy and pressurised lives.

Here then, is the opportunity for a new chapter in the fortunes of Fakenham, which suffered such a stunning blow when its industrial base collapsed in the early 1980s. A number of small print shops were started by former employees and Fakenham still has a range of printing skills. There are some encouraging signs of Fakenham moving ahead on a larger scale.

The Garden Centre, created and run by the Turner family since it was bought by Gordon and Brenda Turner in 1985 and, now they have retired, is run by Martin and Jennie Turner. The racecourse, a success story where David Hunter has been Chief Executive and Clerk of the Course for 19 years. Pensthorpe Natural Park, now the domain of Debs and Bill Jordan, has become a nationally acclaimed award winning destination, and for three years was home to BBC Television's *Springwatch*. Drifters is the town's iconic fish and ship shop operating from an iconic building in Oak Street and whose reputation stretches well beyond Fakenham. Willie Parker, whose family has been established in the town since 1840 and has occupied the last of the traditional shops in Norwich Street since 1890. Tim Aldiss, whose family business has been synonymous with Fakenham and Norfolk since 1892. He is a great fisherman and can persuade a milk fish, which lives on plankton in the Indian Ocean, to suck a fishing fly into its mouth and be caught by rod and line, skill and patience. The market, every Thursday, is one of the best in the county, typified by the Benbow family and Jean Seppings. Fakenham had a very effective policeman for nearly 25 years in PC Sid Wright who had his own style, which was decidedly *non pc (non politically correct)*. He was highly respected.

These and the other characters in the book, John Plummer, Kathy Christianson, Di Braithwaite, Denise Pearson and Brigitte and Stephen Doughty are a really interesting cross section who represent the beating heart of the town as it faces challenge and an exciting future. The expansion implies change but Fakenham's history since the Domesday Book shows it does not shrink from challenge, though it may take its time to grasp it.

The history of Fakenham has some remarkable features, not least that it introduced the second workers' co-operative in the UK. Tim Aldiss and Willie Parker who put me in touch with Nancy McGrath's son, Jimmy, recall: In the 1960s Jimmy Reid, the communist shop steward of Upper Clyde Shipbuilders, declared a workers' take over and formed the first workers' co-operative. In Fakenham there was a long established shoe and handbag factory whose owners, based in Norwich, decided to close down. This was situated on the site of the Old Congregational church in Norwich Road. There was a serious prospect of considerable job loss, which would be sorely felt in the town. The supervisor at the factory in Fakenham, and subsequently its spokesperson and organiser, Mrs Nancy McGrath, determined to fight for continued jobs of the girls employed there. She stood out for them, and set up the second workers' co-operative in the UK, inspired by Jimmy Reid's example.

However, where Jimmy Reid was highly political, her only motivation was to save the jobs of the workers and she organised a sit in. This event, and her spirited stand, attracted attention from politicians and press, but became a political cause which she never intended.

The workers' co-operative had the tools, raw material and experience to make a range of leather and suede goods. This was before the age of web sites, and sales relied on word of mouth and goodwill from former customers and sympathetic wellwishers. However, after a few years when the media had tried to cast her as a political firebrand, the venture became over politicised, which obscured the original idea and it gradually fell apart.

* * *

A famous son of Fakenham was **Sir George Edwards M P.** Born in 1850, he rose from being a farm boy to become a Member of Parliament. He is remembered for his work in founding and running a union for agricultural workers. Knighted by King George V, he lived in Hempton and latterly in Fakenham. He died in 1933, is buried in the Queen's Road cemetery and commemorated on the town sign. (*ref E. M. Bridges, Fakenham-Lancaster 2010*)

_ * _ * _ * _

The Rev'd Adrian Bell was Rector of Fakenham for 10 years and brought about a remarkable transformation at the huge, imposing, parish church. It was built in 1370 with Trinity College, Cambridge as its patron and is a Grade 1 listed building. *(Ref Raymond Monbiot, North Norfolk Living 2011)*

When Adrian came to Fakenham from Lincolnshire he found the doors of the church habitually locked and chained and a parish newsletter with a readership of 300. His early focus was to make the building part of the community. He and the team gradually developed activity in the church so that every day there was something of interest in which his team of helpers could participate and be recognised for their dedication and loyalty. So successful was this objective that numbers of visitors reached 50,000 a year. Seldom fewer than 500 per week were using the church and on average 100 attended services by the end of his tenure. The parish newsletter, now *The Beacon,* has a readership of 10,000, attracts 12 pages of advertising, and is delivered free in the town.

The church has become a destination for coach parties, particularly on market day when it is packed with regular visitors. Its coffee shop providing food and beverages makes £400 per week which is half the parish share.

There are clean loos, books, new and second hand, post cards and souvenirs are always on sale and, once a month jigsaws are exchanged. Charities and organisations have been made welcome to raise money and reach out to the community. He organised a weekly art group, a monthly craft market, a parent and toddler services and children's activities. The church has an annual horticultural show and link with schools to make musical evenings. There is a choir of 20. The highlight of the church's charitable fund raising is the Christmas Tree Festival each December when over 70 separate charities each decorate a Christmas tree and the event raises some £30,000 for their funds. The trees are donated each year by the Fakenham Garden Centre.

Adrian took the view that few churches achieve comparable service to the community. In many towns and villages they are struggling causing great stress to the clergy involved, particularly younger priests who tend to burn out before reaching their potential.

Adrian Bell advocated the return of the Minster approach where a major church, almost like a mini cathedral such as Fakenham, Wells and Walsingham, has daughter churches affiliated and a ministry team with specific authority. As it is, the incumbent does not receive supervisory help and has to deal with whatever comes.

_ * _ * _ * _

Another well known and well loved character was **Sid Hooks** whose cockerels and chickens have run freely for over 50 years in Sandy Lane at Goggs Mill, Hempton, on the shores of the Wensum river. This has brought joy to successive generations of children and earned him the title of Mr Cock a doodle Oo. His cockerels strutted among hens of all shapes, sizes and colours often with baby chicks at mother's feet. *(ref Raymond Monbiot, North Norfolk Living 2008)*

It all started some 50 years ago when Sid and his wife Lillian were persuaded by their daughter to let her rear some chicks. They asked well known Holkham gamekeeper Basil Goffin if he could help. He provided 13 chicks and a mother hen to set up the venture. At peak this grew to about 100 chickens - some 40 hens and 60 cockerels which, unsurprisingly, fought each other noisily and disturbed the hens. Feeding this huge brood has become a destination. Mother ducks and their broods join in the feast. There is a pen and fenced area with hen houses where the chickens have long been encouraged to lay their eggs and keep out of harm's way of foxes at night, however, the emphasis is on free range and overspill into neighbouring fields and the river bank is inevitable as the flock has grown.

Sid hooks was born in Fakenham some 94 years ago. He served in the 5th Royal Norfolk Regiment from the start of the Second World War.

They were deployed to Singapore where he was taken prisoner by the Japanese for three and a half years and was forced to work on the Railway of Death as far as the Bridge on the River Kwai. He had spent 7 days hiding in the jungle with three bullets in his arm and another lodged internally, before he was captured. When he was released from captivity at the end of the war he weighed 6 stone.

When he left the army he worked as an electrical contractor on strategic installations such as aerodromes and the Fylingdales early warning establishment on the Yorkshire moors. He later started a taxi service in Fakenham which he ran for 20 years until he gave up at the age of 80 in 2002.

Raymond Monbiot

By the same author:

The Burnhams Book of Characters and Memories

Characters of North Norfolk

MORE Characters of North Norfolk

Retirement is for Younger People

Acknowledgements

Tim Aldiss

Archant - EDP

Nigel Benbow

Peter Bird

Diana Black

Dr E M Bridges

Ian Burt

Brigitte Doughty

Richard Denyer

Roger Harris

Delia Malim-Robinson

Jimmy McGrath

North Norfolk Living

Willie Parker

Carla Phillips

Richard Powell

Julian Sturdy

Matthew Usher

Jane Wright

About the Author

Raymond Monbiot was born in Kent in 1937 and educated at Westminster School. He was a schoolmaster for a while and taught nine- year- olds Latin, history and English at a prep school. He found that Latin could be taught more effectively by engaging a more contemporary theme than can be found in *Kennedy's Latin Primer.* So, he set the class to work translating nursery rhymes, for example,

Sedebat in muro Humptios Dumptios,
Collapsus est muro Humptios Dumptios,
Et regis equi et regis viri componere possent,
Humptium Dumptium.

They also translated parts of *The Gondoliers.* The better the behaviour and aptitude, the bigger the parts allocated, and it was performed before amazed parents at the end of term.

In1956 he entered the food industry as a trainee with J. Lyons & Co, humping sacks of flour in the basement of Cadby Hall in west London.

These were formative years for learning to understand people. By the age of nineteen he was foreman on the night shift in the bread bakery at a time when the foreman had authority. In later years this authority was delegated to the human resources department.

The foreman had responsibility for motivating employees, many of them casual, who had enrolled for the night from the local doss house in Hammersmith, looking for an opportunity to sleep in the warm rather than work. The factory was a Victorian building, six storeys high, and in the course of his duties Raymond was the target of a 44lb tin of frozen egg thrown from the roof and of a 500lb barrel of fat rolled down the stairs. Both missed their target but made an indelible impression none the less. Despite these incidents involving the casuals, the challenge was to get the job done to time and standard, and the loyalty and dedication of the many long-term employees was truly impressive. The war had not long ended and family men and women were trying to recreate some stability and normality. It was a humbling, but indispensable experience, to learn that security and recognition for effort are the best motivators.

Raymond was trained as a pastry chef making, among other things, cakes for Buckingham Palace garden parties and fruit scones, by hand, for the Queen Mother's breakfast. He chose to move on to the sales side of the business and started as a van salesman, selling and delivering cake to a round of shops. He worked his way up the sales ladder to sales director, and eventually ran three food companies for Lyons as managing director. After 22 years he was headhunted to be managing director of Associated Biscuits, then comprising Jacobs, Peek Freans and Huntley & Palmers. In 1982 he moved to Campbells Soups as chairman UK. In 1988 he founded his own food consultancy business.

He was an active member of the Conservative Party for over 54 years and held every volunteer position except chairman of the women's organisation. He was the senior volunteer 2003 to 2006 and deputy chairman of the party, and from 2006 to 2011 a treasurer and chairman of its property company. Awarded MBE 1981, and CBE 1994, he declined a life peerage in 2010. The years involved with the Conservative Party brought him into contact with every one of its leaders since Winston Churchill, and many senior ministers. The cut and thrust of parliamentary debate has not improved since television made it into popular entertainment, encouraging 'yah boo' politics. Memorable repartee, however, remains in his mind.

Harold Macmillan was being taunted by a northern railwayman MP about hunting and shooting. He thanked the MP for his observations but said he would value his opinion more on shunting and hooting. Iain Mcleod, one of the great losses to politics through his early death, proposed a bargain with one of his tormentors: 'You stop telling lies about me and I'll stop telling the truth about you.' However, the sharpest lines were by no means monopolised by the Conservatives as witness the barbs of Dennis Skinner, aka the 'Beast of Bolsover' and by Denis Healey.

One of Raymond's most exacting tasks was to chair the Conservative party conference in the year 2000. With thousands in the hall, and many more watching on television, the challenge over four days was to get the audience on side and keep them there. One splendid councillor, addressing the gathering, started her speech with, 'You don't frighten me, I've got children...' There were 300,000 members of the party in those days with many different opinions about what should be done. In his three years as chairman of the volunteers there were three different leaders and four party chairmen, each of whom expected a transfer of loyalty in his or her direction – not an easy task at times.

Married to Rosalie Monbiot OBE, they have two surviving children: George, a well known environmentalist who writes for the *Guardian,* and Eleanor, a senior director of World Vision who lives in Kenya and was awarded the OBE at the age of 34. Their daughter Katherine died at the age of 31. Raymond and Rosalie moved to Norfolk in 2000. Rosalie was elected a Norfolk county councillor and to the parish council. She has been a school governor for over 50 years.

The Monbiots planted an orchard of heritage apple trees at their home in Burnham Market and are keenly interested in cultivating them. They established a unique burr knot apple tree, that is one resulting from a cutting rather than from grafting, which can produce apples unlike the variety from which the cutting was obtained. This planting produced just such an apple and it was named Canon Cooke after Rosalie's brother, Hereward.

They celebrated their golden wedding with the help of 100 friends in 2011. Raymond is a published author. His first book, *'How to Manage Your Boss'*, sold 30,000 copies. He was a regular contributor to trade magazines and since moving to Norfolk writes features on interesting people for *North Norfolk Living*. He has written four books about Norfolk characters for whom he has a lot of respect.

The first was *The Burnhams Book of Characters*, followed by *Characters of North Norfolk* and by *MORE Characters of North Norfolk*. The latest is *Characters of Fakenham*. He contributed a chapter to *The Return of the Tide,* and was one of the team who wrote *The Book of the Burnhams.* He compiled and published *Retirement is for Younger People,* which reflects his respect for the volunteers who carry on contributing their energy and experience to the community, regardless of their age. One couple were still delivering meals on wheels aged 86.

A former chairman of the Burnhams Society, he is a keen gardener and specialises in roses as far as the soil and climate allow. Wherever they have lived he and Rosalie have planted a mulberry tree. He has won numerous prizes for rose growing and he and Rosalie encourage barn owls and hedgehogs at Eastgate House, Burnham Market.

CHARACTERS OF FAKENHAM

Jean Seppings

Where can you buy the best carrot cake in Norfolk? Jean Seppings makes it, and sells her range of homemade cakes and pastries from her unique trailer each Thursday at the Fakenham market. There is a signature of quality and freshness about all her products, from her sausage rolls with their crisp pastry and plenty of succulent filling, to her quiches and pies. Her coffee walnut cake and crunchy flapjacks are in a class of their own.

"Tuesday and Wednesday are my baking days preparing for an early start on Thursday market day. Early? ...around 5.00 am. There is a growing demand for portions of cake for people living alone. Their numbers are increasing and it is nice to supply some comfort to elderly and lonely people, many of whom I have known for years."

Jean is a good hearted, caring person and seldom without an appreciative long- term customer chatting to her while she's working. Well known in Fakenham, she bought the wine bar, behind the cinema, in 1991 and ran it for fourteen years. She developed it into a successful bistro with a range of homemade food which was unique in the town. "At one time we had more than twenty staff and were busy most of the time but particularly on a Thursday morning and Saturday evening. I also ran two coffee shops for Tim Aldiss, one in the store which later was destroyed in the awful fire that ravaged that part of the town, and one in the furniture store.

"Ten years ago I felt it was time for a change. It was a hard decision to make as I had seen so many changes, having all my children grow up and work in the restaurant, but it was the right thing for me to do.

Jean married David 35 years ago and they have three children. David had a long history at the butcher's shop which was in Raynham. "We lived for two or three years in Kettlestone and then moved to Fakenham where there was more for the children to do as they grew up.

"We have two girls: Louise, who works for Virgin Airlines at Heathrow, and Victoria, who works in Les Mill's gym in New Zealand – used for training by the All Blacks, not that she attributes their Rugby World Cup success wholly to that and Jonathan is responsible for water sports at Woburn. David has worked for many years for FMC harvesters, now PMC, and this took him away from time to time. Running the business and bringing up three children made for a very full life. When I sold the wine bar I was looking for something less demanding to do.

"For two years I tried working for other people but did not like my loss of freedom. I found outside catering absorbing and supplied catering lines, notably to Liam at The Galley, who was ex Bistro. Then I went on to the market in Fakenham, selling homemade cakes and pastries, starting with a stall and later using our custom- made trailer, pioneered with David's help, which took less setting- up time each market day. I also have a display table to set out my range of quiches - (which people call quirky), pies, pastries, loaf- shaped and portioned cakes.

"I was approached by Trudi at the racecourse who suggested that I might sell my range at race meetings. This I have done for a number of years and the recent developments at the course have enabled a move into a new well- sheltered location in the mainstream.

"There are noticeable changes in demand such as the growth of gluten free and dairy free. Consumers are not short of advice on what to eat and what to avoid these days although much of it is conflicting. But cake is largely comfort food and demand for less of certain ingredients may be the way consumers persuade themselves to continue buying and enjoying cakes and pastries.

"I am still busy with catering for events. I cook regularly for the rugby club and for the gym as well as private parties and funerals but not weddings – they are too demanding. I prepare Christmas dinner for the old people's sheltered home. I am always amazed how much they can eat. It is an enormous three-course meal and everything is eaten up followed by a singalong."

Jean was born in Lincolnshire at Sutton Bridge, near where the butterfly farm is now. Her ancestors worked the land for generations in Lincolnshire. Her father was a prisoner of war in Burma. When she left school she spent a year at college in Ely on a secretarial course and later worked in offices in Long Sutton. But her flair for cooking led her career in that direction.

It is fair to say that the main changes in Jean's career were not planned. Opportunities occurred and she had the vision and courage to grasp them. This was not without risk but at each stage she brought her capacity for hard work and talent to bear and has earned a reputation for producing the best on a constant basis.

A keen golfer, she plays off a 17 handicap twice a week all the year round if possible and three to four times a week in the summer. Each year there is the challenge of the Greenkeeper's Revenge, where the most difficult course is laid out with the pins put in the most awkward places; for example, one on a hill where a shortfall sees the ball rolling back, or if over hit sees it rolling the other way, seemingly for ever. Jean was ladies' captain of the golf club for two years. She likes to play golf wherever she and David are on holiday.

So what lies ahead?
"David and I are looking to enjoy life. We have holidayed all over the world and particularly like the Victoria Falls. We want to do some more of that, fitting it in to what will continue to be a busy life."

David Hunter

David Hunter combines the roles of Chief Executive and Clerk of the Course at Fakenham racecourse. It is unusual for these roles to be combined in one person but David is never one to avoid a challenge. It requires a well-judged and consistent balance between the aspirations of owners, trainers, jockeys and racegoers. The success of Fakenham racing, up from six meetings a year to the present thirteen, is testimony to his effectiveness. Fakenham is a well-loved local course for all that it is remote from much of Britain, surrounded on three sides by sea and a left-handed course just a mile circuit. So how have David Hunter and his impressive long-serving team created this successful enterprise?

David explains, "There is a quirkiness about Fakenham racing. All staff working for the racecourse company are locals. They are encouraged to be kind, courteous and polite and, where necessary, firm. Our key staff giving the guidance and making sure it happens are Rita in charge of hospitality, Trudi who runs the local staff, and Vivien, all of whom were here when I came nineteen years ago.

"We look after and make it fun for owners and trainers. Our hospitality is exceptional in our custom- built Prince of Wales stand which cost £1.2 million. We raised this with help from a Euro grant, donations and loans from individuals. Making all welcome does much to secure loyalty and support. We have 600 annual members who pay fees of £225 for double or £145 for single. For thirteen race meetings a year this is excellent value. Others who come perhaps two or three times a year have the option to become day members paying £40 for two adults and £8 for parking. They have access to all the members' facilities and the view from the Prince of Wales stand is stunning. Non- members appreciate that they can pay for their parking while in their car.

"One of our long- serving staff is usually manning the turnstile selling entry tickets and racecards. He has the knack of recognising our regulars and exchanging the sort of goodwill that starts the day well. We have spent considerable sums on the infrastructure at the course. The catering is of a high standard and there are facilities for coffee, hog roast, seafood, soup, cakes, and stalls for clothes and accessories.

"Fakenham has a favourable climate for racing. The ground drains well and we can function when other courses are waterlogged or the 'going' too hard. We are basically a winter course operating between October and May. This avoids irrigating in the summer – demand for water in East Anglia with its relatively low rainfall and huge agricultural activity causes restrictions. We have a reputation for honesty and timely information about the 'going' before each race day. Trainers coming from long distances need to know in time what to expect of conditions before they set out. Furthermore a break in the seasons is beneficial. We focus on grade 4, 5 and 6 races and occasionally grade 3. The top of the pyramid such as Cheltenham needs to be underpinned by these grassroots grades which give horses a chance to start a career."

David Hunter was born in Somerset and was educated at King's College, Taunton. His father was a distinguished lawyer in Bristol.

"I never bothered the registrars at universities, and determined to go into the army. I passed into Sandhurst at nineteen and was commissioned in 4th/7th Royal Dragoon Guards. As a green second lieutenant I was guided by my NCOs, who are the finest in the world and the backbone of the army. It proved to be a lesson for life. Working with soldiers is a great leveller. One learns early how to get the best out of them and I loved their bravado. The lesson is as relevant to people outside the army with whom one relates through life. There is more to being an officer than blood, guns and shouting. Recognition of effort and respect will encourage far more co-operation than heavy- handed rank pulling. And if one makes a mistake the way out of it is usually to admit and apologise for it.

"It is about good manners. Regrettably young people, and older ones who should know better, too often forget that. They do not answer invitations, or write letters of thanks or indeed write letters at all, relying sporadically on communicating via e. mail.

"The regiment was equipped with heavy armoured battle tanks and based in Germany in the front line of the Cold War. The threat of nuclear war was very real at that time, facing as we were heavy forces in Eastern Europe. Leave was only granted if you could be back at regimental duty within 24 hours. However, NATO overestimated the strength and intention of these opposing forces. Their equipment was substandard, they feared mass desertions of their troops in the event of war and our nuclear deterrent did much to hold the peace.

"I was a soldier for ten years during which time I was posted to Cyprus twice, running the forces polo team and stables there, and was ADC to Brigadier Andrew Myrtle, the highly professional land forces commander. I was posted to Northern Ireland, commanding troops patrolling the Crumlin Road, and later as second- in- command of a squadron training in Canada. I learnt to ski in Switzerland whilst training and taking part in inter-regimental ski competitions. I was posted to the *Cadre Noir* at the national training school in Samour in the Loire Valley in France, the French equivalent of the Spanish riding school in Vienna. This taught intense high school dressage, the origins of which are in cavalry warfare – as indeed are all the components of the modern pentathlon. I spent eleven months at Samour and most days rode fifteen horses up to five hours a day in total. I returned to the regiment and spent the last two years of my service as an instructor at Sandhurst. I have few regrets in my army career but I would number among them that I did not take advantage of the chance to learn German and I should have tried for selection for the SAS – I probably would not have got in but I should have tried!

"I wanted to be declared redundant from the army under the Option for Change but they would not agree to it. I had been offered another job so I resigned with the rank of captain and joined the International League for the Protection of Horses, a charity based in Snetterton where I stayed for five years. Then I saw the advertisement for a part- time role at Fakenham racecourse for which I applied successfully and moved to Fakenham. Later I also joined the Paralympic Equestrian Dressage twenty-strong team of which I was manager for thirteen years. The focus was on dressage and we had considerable success competing in three Paralympic Games, four world championships and six European championships. And we won team gold medals at all of them. The greatest moment of my life was swearing the oath at the London Paralympics before 85,000 people in the stadium and several millions watching on television.

"Raising money to run and develop a successful racecourse has been a constant challenge. There are five main streams to our fund- raising.

The biggest is the sale of media rights. Then there is our income from the Horseracing Betting Levy Board, followed by the income from attendance, other functions such as food and the most difficult of all, race sponsorship. We aim, and for the most part succeed, in achieving attractive prize money for each race to attract talented entries and jockeys. We also have non- racing income from a caravan site, non-race day functions, private parties and corporate meetings. The ground staff do a fine job in the upkeep of the estate and we attract income from parties and celebrations as a venue of preference.

"I have been very fortunate in the support and help from the directors, of which there are ten. There are nine men and one woman, none of whom have any financial interest in or out, and who support us voluntarily. The chairman, who serves for three years, is appointed by the fellow directors and the vice chairman usually succeeds after that term. I am now on my sixth chairman and every one of them has been a joy to work with. Horse racing is second only to football as the biggest attended sport and is unique in that it has its own dedicated newspaper."

David was married to Adriana for twenty years until they divorced in 2010. They have three children, all of them talented, particularly in music. Hannah went on from Greshams to study English at Newcastle University and is now attending a singing course in London. Max, who was head boy at Greshams, is a very talented guitarist and is setting up a rock band called Martha Gunn. Celia is at the Leys School in Cambridge. She is a fine singer. David maintains that this family musical talent comes from their mother but, as I did not hear him sing, I have no confirmation or otherwise of his contribution to it.

David was awarded an honorary doctorate in civil law at the University of East Anglia. "My father would have been much amused and surprised at this as I had never made any pretensions of being an academic." He dislikes government interference, with such gestures as the hunting ban, and the erosion of that individuality which is the hallmark of Fakenham's success.

Gerald and Denise Benbow

The Benbow home was in Stiffkey. Their father Brian, now approaching his mid-80s, has lived there all his life and is one of the hardest working and most helpful of men who would turn his hand to any challenge. The family is two sons, Nigel and Gerald, and one daughter, Denise.

"Mother sadly died recently," says Gerald. "She had a stroke and never recovered despite months in hospital." We are all involved in the fruit and vegetable business that Brian started from small beginnings. He worked an allotment the other side of the main road from the Stiffkey lamp shop which at the time was a pub."

Brian had greenhouses there and grew lettuces, vegetables and chrysanthemums. On Friday evenings he and his family would call on every house in the village selling them his fresh produce. They knew everyone from one end of the village to the other. Forty years ago the council offered Brian a new site at Camping Hill in Stiffkey. He moved everything there and carried on the business.

Gerald explains, "He had up to five jobs on the go. He rode a Lambretta, safely for most of the time, except when he met a patch of oil on the road returning to Stiffkey from Aylsham on one occasion. He fell off and the skid broke his ankle. Of more concern was that he squashed the six peaches he was carrying in a bag. One of Brian's five jobs was bait digging and he continued doing this with a broken ankle."

Denise remembers, "At one time he had bought an Austin 7 for £125. He did not have a driving licence at the time but drove it nonetheless. He sold it later for what he paid for it. He dug graves, was a postman and would respond to any request for help. It was not unusual for us to have a knock on the door at night and be asked if he could dig a grave tomorrow, always by hand and in any of the different soils of the district. I can remember his comments about digging in Wighton cemetery where it was hard chalk soil.

"Gradually he opened shops to sell fruit and vegetables and had six of them at one time. These were at Aylsham, two in Cromer, Sheringham, Holt and Fakenham. This was a heavy commitment for the family and with father not getting any younger, we reduced the number of shops initially to a more manageable three, at Fakenham, Holt and Cromer, and have since shut Cromer.

"We were all born in Stiffkey and went to the village school until they closed it. Then we went on to Wells which we reached by bus. I think we all learned a lot more since leaving school than ever we did there. There was not a lot to do in Stiffkey. It was a small village with few amenities and we did not have the transport or the money to take us further afield. So we had to make our own pleasures. We spent a lot of time on the marshes swimming and playing hide and seek. We went beach combing which, before the coming of containers, gave good pickings after a storm at sea when deck cargoes were washed overboard and fetched up along the shore line. There was some good timber to be had in those days."

Gerald takes up the story: "We went fishing for trout and eels in the River Stiffkey. We used wool, impregnated with worms and tied on to our fishing lines to catch eels. They have very sharp teeth which got caught in the wool, and could be hauled in. We gathered samphire and winkles and found empty artillery shells left over from the war washed up on the beach but cannot recall any live ammunition.

"We picked strawberries and blackcurrants in the school holidays and there were wild mushrooms around if you knew where to find them. We played a lot in the street outside each others' houses.

"Nigel was always good with his hands, particularly with anything electrical. He teamed up with Wayne Scoles for electrical projects and their teacher gave them an old washing machine which they took apart. The teacher said he did not tell them to do that but as they had done so they had better put it together again. And it worked. If you have working hands you can always find a day's work."

Gerald continues: "Bait digging was the main occupation at Stiffkey but Father advised us not to make it a career. However, both Nigel and I spent years bait digging. It was well organised. Harry Bishop used to load them up in a transit van and take them for distribution by rail to fishing centres around the coastline. Some days his van was so tightly packed that he had to remove all but the driving seat to fit them in. A transit van full of worms is a lot of worms. We felt we were making our contribution to nature when after our digging the little birds would flock in to pick up the bits and pieces that they would not have found had we not been there.

"Bait digging is a lonely job even though there were many of us out there at low tide. We were paid by the hundred and had to count the worms as we dug them. This did not make for much conversation but it sharpened our skill to keep numbers in our heads which was of benefit later in a shopkeeping life. Harry Bishop had thirteen diggers working for him and he would buy their worms at so much a hundred. The busy months were the cod season from September to December when we might each dig 1500 worms a day. We worked at it on average five hours a day.

"We liked to go butt forking for fish at low tide. Warham Drift is a gully or low drain on the Stiffkey marshes with a bank at one end that prevented the fish from escaping. It was a very productive patch to go after flatfish. The favourite instrument was a butt fork made of shark hooks which Bill Gidney the blacksmith straightened out and made it into a sort of trident. It was not unusual to catch 200 fish with one of these. We also stretched long lines with hooks every 18 inches parallel with the incoming tide. We baited up the hooks and covered them with sand to protect them from seabirds before they were covered by the sea. When the tide went out there would be pools along the line where the fish caught by the hooks would burrow down.

"As bait diggers we had to take the rough with the smooth. Demand for bait fell away with the scarcity of fish after Christmas and we could sell only 300- 400 worms a day in the next few months. So it was hard to make a living from bait digging all the year round.

"Yet people were happy with village life. It was limited by today's standards but we appreciated what we had. We were happier than many people with much more money and many more possessions are today. The more you have the more you want. The village hall was the centre of activity in Stiffkey as there was no pub at the time. There was weekly bingo and events during the year. We played cricket and there was the annual fete which brought in a lot of visitors."

After ten years as a bait digger Nigel came in to the family fruit and vegetable business full time running the Fakenham shop. Brian still buys the flowers and plants, Gerald buys the vegetables and Denise buys the fruit. At one time Brian would make the round trip to Covent Garden

Nigel Benbow

regularly, starting out at 3.00 a.m.   He still goes to Spalding to buy flowers. Benbows have always favoured local produce when they can obtain it.   But gradually small growers have closed down or contracted to the supermarkets.

As Denise says: " At one time we had a choice of five strawberry growers but few are left in the area now.   Consumers have become used to buying any product at any time of year.   There are sprouts imported from Australia, carrots from Tasmania and apples from New Zealand. However, we still have the edge on the supermarkets in local products. Fenland celery in season is unbeatable. We buy strawberries, asparagus, sprouts, carrots, beetroot and potatoes whenever these are available locally. They are delivered fresh and direct without going halfway round the world or through a lengthy distribution system. We display seasonal local products outside the shops."

Gerald and Denise run a busy market stall at the Fakenham market every Thursday and at Sheringham market on a Saturday. It is a major feature of the town in Fakenham on market day and represents the real Norfolk. The customers are getting older as it is a way of life not experienced by many younger shoppers who want their food wrapped and ready. Many young people cannot cook these days so there is no benefit to them to buy produce in the raw which they have to prepare, peel, cut and cook from scratch. As the market day customers get older so their needs must be available. One of these needs is that many of them as they get older are lonely and dislike the confusion and pace of the supermarkets where they have limited opportunity to talk with a sympathetic shopkeeper. Gerald and Denise provide friendly contact with their customers, many of them regulars.

It is hard work running a market stall. For Gerald and Denise setup time is about three and a half hours in all weathers to be ready for the customers by 8.30 a.m. "Some get there earlier. So on market day we arrive at our pitch at 5.00 a.m. However, before that the vehicle has to be loaded with last- minute products so it cannot all be done the evening before. The stall has to be built from metal scaffolding and the produce displayed. Then at the end of the day it takes over an hour to dismantle and clear away. Little wonder there are few younger stall- holders setting up."
In Britain there are some 5/600,000 unfilled jobs but young people complain that they cannot find work. Employers will say if you give a young Brit work the likelihood of his or her turning up each day is limited and the jobs go to those who want them – often immigrants who will stick at it.

Gerald, who went to the Norfolk School of Horticulture, has had a plant nursery in Briston for the last 15 years specialising in hardy herbaceous plants. This is Dover Farm Nurseries and when he is on market duty his wife Louise runs it. They have a daughter and three grandsons. Denise runs the Holt shop with Susan who has been engaged to Nigel for 30 years. Denise has been engaged for a similar time to Susan's brother Stephen.

Benbows is very much a family business and maintains the best of Norfolk traditions. There is no let- up seven days a week and none of them have ever taken a holiday. And they don't just offer produce for sale. A visit to Nigel's shop is as good a cabaret as one will find for miles around. There is always chat and many customers who have already been served will stay around for the entertainment. There is no problem about joining in. The shops have a loyal and long- serving staff who are almost part of the family. Gerald and Denise's market stall makes a similar offering and is never short of a laugh. The Benbows are good for Fakenham.

Brigitte and Stephen Doughty

Brigitte's father was an RAF pilot who was deployed to West Raynham in 1972. He had served in many parts of the world and Brigitte by the age of twelve had been to eleven schools. They had lived in Cyprus where her father had flown Canberras and Vulcan bombers. Now he was looking for stability for his family of wife and three children and uninterrupted education. They came to live in Fakenham. He died aged 53. Tragically her brother, to whom she was very close, was also later to die of a brain tumour at 45. Her mother Bobbie Wood is going strong and as bubbly as ever.

Says Brigitte: "When I left school I worked as a secretary in the office of the Marquess Townshend's Raynham Farms and among my duties at Christmas time was the delivery of braces of pheasants in feather across his estate. I was given a brace but I really did not know how to deal with them.

"I studied foot care on a course at Maidenhead College. It was a useful introduction to medical anatomy and physiology. At nineteen I wanted to be an air hostess but could not do so under the age of 21. However, before I reached that age I met Stephen who was my husband to be. We were married in Fakenham church in 1983 but we did not have the money for a honeymoon at the time– I dug the garden instead. Before Stephen started his own practice he worked for the North Norfolk District Council on architectural and planning projects. He is Fakenham born and bred.

"Stephen was very ill with a brain tumour 25 years ago. This took a serious toll on his health at the time and meant that we should work from home. We had the pavilion where I ran a bed and breakfast for a while but my interest in matters of the feet made that a well-favoured and practical career move which enabled me to work based at home. I set up in practice as a foot health practitioner. Word of mouth set the practice going and I have become busier with every passing year. Looking after patients' feet means dealing with people who are pleased to relax and often confide to a willing listener. Most of my customers are regulars whom I see perhaps once every six weeks as their nails grow and their feet require attention. I am comfortable with the role of mother confessor and happy if patients want to tell me their problems.

"At one time I wanted to join the police force but I am too much of a softie to make a success of that. I do home visits and work closely with the Royal British Legion in Cromer. Perhaps at times I stretch the call of duty, doing the shopping for older and disabled patients, but it is all about building lasting relationships. For the last twenty years I have helped raise funds for cancer charities and on my 50th birthday we had nearly 200 guests who donated £1500 in total for a brain tumour charity in memory of my brother who died eight years before. A memorial rugby match is held on an annual basis. Funds raised go to nominated local charities.

"We have three children: Jonathan, who works in Stephen's practice and has two children, Georgina, who lives and works in Norwich, and William,

our youngest, is sixteen. I like to spend time with the grandchildren when I get a day off. It is a break from the routine and a joy to see them grow up."

Stephen's work brings him into contact with clients, developers and council planners. There is a focus on new build, barn conversions and commercial buildings. He is less enthusiastic about extensions. He says: "These can be very frustrating at times, they take longer than originally planned and sometimes crowd out other more interesting work. Second-homers are changing the profile of the area particularly on the northern coastline. It has become a matter of debate as to the pros and cons of the second- home owner. Some say there are major economic benefits to be had, whilst locals bemoan the fact that they can no longer afford property in their local villages.

"The plans for expansion in the town will be beneficial. The 800 new houses in the north of Fakenham means an increase in population of perhaps 3000. This will need shops and infrastructure, new amenities and recreation. Fakenham has a lot going for it. There is the Thursday market which is one of the best in the county, we have a river, racecourse and are well sited for communications.

"We need to bring back the railway which was a vital link years ago between towns. I used regularly to catch the train to Wells, where my father was born and where my grandmother still lived and had a beach hut. We need to see the circular route restored. Most of the bridges are still there and the track route largely available and could be re-laid. There is a plan but it is not very ambitious. Yet the country is planning to spend vast sums on high-speed rail and new trackways. A portion of that diverted to Norfolk would transform the area."

I asked Stephen why, if the outlook is so favourable, Fakenham has missed out in its range of shops and facilities compared to Dereham or Holt, and why the remaining small shops and the market traders are in pessimistic mood. What employment opportunities will there be for this growing population or will they have to go further afield to find work?

Stephen responded: "The main industry used to be printing, employing thousands of people, and it collapsed all of a sudden with a mass of redundancies. This was not planned and the town was left to its own devices. Norwich Street used to be bustling with a range of shops, for example two hardware shops where you could get any hardware item – if prepared to wait while rummaging through the stock went on. It was real 'four candles/fork handles' time. Now both shops are closed. There was a 'Home and Colonial's store and businesses which had been there for decades; Willie Parker's clock shop is the sole remainder of that era. The availability of labour brings investment and Fakenham will be open for new business as it expands. The Crown Hotel, which used to be the gateway to the Market Place is re-opening, the site of the burnt-out Aldiss store will be rebuilt with three storeys and diversified attractions. I am hopeful for the future of Fakenham.

"Growing up in the town had mainly happy memories. We worked for the young people in the community, and when I was sixteen to eighteen I was the youngest qualified youth leader in Norfolk, ever. We laboured mightily, and raised enough money for a purpose-built youth club and pavilion adjacent to the police station. It was a great sadness when it was shut down for other development.

We saw our timber and brickwork demolished overnight and just lying in piles to be cleared away.

"We would get up to youthful pranks. For example, tying black cotton to a dead mouse and drawing it through the streets from a distance to make it look alive. We did a newspaper and rag collection service and took them to Richardsons which was where the laundry is now. This paid us some pocket money as did the car wash we operated at two shillings and sixpence a car. We would help the market stall-holders take down their structures after a day's work. They used Tilly lamps at the time and I can still smell their distinctive aroma. We picked strawberries and blackcurrants in season. We always had money and we wasted it.

"I still see former school pals around the town whom I have known since the age of six. I went on a memorable trip with the grammar school to Speyer in Germany, and conversed in pidgin German, which I largely made up. I was amazed that there was a bar in the school for the benefit of the pupils who, in British terms, were all under age drinkers. I could have done better at school to realise my potential, particularly in my favourite subjects of geography and history, but I was too interested in sport. I have long been a supporter of Fakenham football club, laughed with them and fundraised for them.

"My father was a public health inspector and, later, deputy surveyor in Walsingham. He had a remarkable gift for making or repairing anything. He refurbished a Triumph Thunderbird sports car and it took him three years to get it to perfect condition. It still exists in a garage in Fakenham.

"There is a belief that planning permission is easier to get nowadays. The truth is that it is twice as difficult as it was ten years ago, with ever increasing new hurdles to overcome. The insistence on affordable housing, as part of new developments, is just one of them. Building a £100,000 house, in the midst of a development of homes which sell for £600,000, does not come easily. It can be organised, however, by arranging for affordable houses to be built elsewhere and not in the middle of expensive new properties. So the number of affordable houses dictated by government can be met – but not here. It is the same mindset as selling excess carbon emissions to countries with low levels and who can notionally absorb them for a fee. This all takes time and causes delay. It is typical of politics today where headline-grabbing gestures and political expediency, have switched off my enthusiasm to the extent that I have not voted for any party for the last four elections.

"At one time I fancied becoming a doctor. I attended a massage course and then my health problems intervened.

"As to the future I would like to wind down a bit. In our two acres of garden we used to grow vegetables and flowers. The spread of the muntjac was unhelpful to both and we have reverted to nature with grass and trees. However, it is still too much – the ground seems to get further away from one's hands and knees as the years pass.. Brigitte walks our cocker spaniel, Poppy. We had a golden setter for many years.

John Plummer

John and Pat Plummer

"My great, grandfather, Robert Leech Plummer, was a remarkable man. His courage and good fortune enabled successive generations to exist and thrive. He was a beachman and fisherman at Caistor and he jumped ship to go on the gold rush in Australia on sailing ships. On his return he was one of the survivors of the *Zephyr* yawl disaster in 1885 which killed eight of the fifteen on board. His father, my great, great, grandfather, was also a beachman and fisherman, which was a dangerous but lucrative occupation. In 1869 he sold a share in his Caistor beach company for £100, the equivalent of many £thousands today.

"My father, William Robert, was born in Great Yarmouth as was my mother. He was a chartered accountant. I was born in Hellesdon in 1948 and went to Heather Avenue junior school where there were 52 in my class. When I passed my eleven+ I went to the City of Norwich

School which was an excellent grammar school with a fine record of sending pupils to Cambridge University. There were good and enthusiastic teachers for local studies. I enjoyed a year of music but biology, science and games were my favourites. I had the advantage from an early age of knowing the direction I wanted my career to take. I had an uncle who was a dentist and I resolved to be either a dentist or a doctor.

"I went on to Manchester University in 1967 and qualified in dentistry in 1972. I made some wonderful friends and have kept in touch with a number of them, having several reunions over the years. One of them was Alan Segal who, at the time when cross- infection control was in its infancy, developed a disposable three- in- one syringe. This became a significant advance at a time when professional standards were being brought up to date. Alan benefited mightily and deservedly.

"Dental student life was hard work but also enjoyable and exciting and I have many happy memories of these times. And, of course, being able to watch George Best, Dennis Law and Bobby Charlton regularly at Old Trafford – an added bonus - was something I'll never forget.

"My first job was houseman at the dental school and then at Manchester Royal Infirmary. Its location was close to the Moss Side district where fractured jaws were not unusual and once led to the daunting experience of having to testify as an expert witness in the Crown Court. Then I went into practice at Poynton in the Cheshire stockbroker belt – quite a change from Moss Side. Gradually my friends dispersed to take up new appointments and locations and I felt it was time to move back to East Anglia. In 1974 I went to work in Lowestoft for Ian Fox who was a wonderful dentist, taught me a lot and fortunately made light of my bachelor excesses. Despite his liking for country music (not my taste) he was nevertheless an inspirational figure. It was in Lowestoft that a neighbour introduced me to the music of the rhythm and blues band Dr Feelgood. I became a fan straightaway and still am.

"In 1978 I decided to join the dental practice in Fakenham which for many years was located in the attractive building that now houses Drifters fish and chip shop. At first I lived in Holt, where during a brief marriage and divorce my first son Duncan was born. He is now mayor of Holt and is married to Nina. Both are chartered accountants and have two daughters, Isabelle and Eleanor. I was captain of the Holt cricket club at this time and had to give a speech at the annual dinner but had no one to go with. One of my team mates, the local butcher, suggested that his sister- in- law, Pat, might be pleased to accompany me. That blind date developed most happily and Pat and I were married in 1983. It was the best move I ever made and it's all down to that team mate Graham who is now my brother- in- law.

"Pat was PA to Sir Timothy Colman, then Lord Lieutenant of Norfolk, and we moved to live in Fakenham in 1984. Pat and I have two children: Kate, who is now a research ecologist specialising in the effects of feeding garden birds and who has broadcast on the subject on BBC Radio 4, and Patrick who taught geography at Greshams and now lives in Melbourne, Australia. Pat was a magistrate from 1991 to 2014 in Norwich and district and sat as a chairman in both adult and youth courts. As well as running a dental practice, I started and ran a short tennis coaching group for four-

to eight-year-olds for several years and then helped as a coach at Fakenham cricket club. Both these activities were very rewarding, if a little hectic, but it is great to see so many of the children I used to coach still enjoying and playing those games to a high standard as adults.

"We moved into Fakenham in 1984. We celebrated my 30th anniversary of the dental practice in 2008 in my old surgery at Drifters with former colleagues.

"I am always cycling around the town, sometimes erratically, on one occasion attracting a police siren to find it was PC Sid Wright driving the police car, and when he passed me he pointed his finger and mouthed with a big laugh, 'Got ya'"

One of my scariest experiences was to climb up the tower of Fakenham parish church with David Carr whose responsibility it was to run up the flag on special days such as St George's Day, the Queen's birthday, etc, and take it down at night. The stairs were nearly vertical, there was no handrail and when one reached the top and emerged on to the roof there was only a low railing to stop one making a very much more rapid descent. One frosty night David awoke, agitated that he had forgotten to take down the flag. So he climbed up the tower in the dark to find that he had in fact taken it down earlier but it had been a convivial evening and he had no recollection of having done so. There was a wonderful view up there and I have to thank David for the pictures which I enlarged and stuck on card to the ceiling of the treatment room so patients would have something interesting to look at and distract them from the treatment. One day the card detached itself from the ceiling and the patient noticed it before I did and started moving about. It fell, showering some debris.

"I had lots of young patients and would give diet advice at their check-ups warning of the dangers of eating too many sweets. Several of these children, including my daughter, went to Sylvia's ballet school where lessons ended with sweets. Once when I took my three- year- old son with me to collect her I refused to let him have any sweets and, with several of my patients and their mothers watching, he threw a tantrum. Seldom have I been so embarrassed, having to deal with the sort of behaviour that I was forever telling mums to resist.

"I had some colourful characters as patients. One, a farmer with a heart of gold, had a reputation for unparalleled rudeness and treated me with no exception. One day I said I had hit upon a money- raising scheme. There was a view of my treatment room from the garden from where it was possible to look inside for anyone so minded and I suggested that we sell tickets for a view of him having dental treatment. We would make a fortune as all of Fakenham would buy a ticket. Another patient, who was usually on time, was half an hour late for her appointment. I asked why she was late and she said she had been watching the snooker on the telly and did not want to miss the end of it.

"Another patient came in with toothache and I said the tooth should come out. He begged me to find a way to save it and with reluctance I said it was 'split or bust' (or words to that effect) if I performed a root canal procedure to try to save it. Some time later he came again and said the treatment had been successful but he had another tooth in the same state as the first one. Could I give him some more 'split or bust' treatment?

"And another patient once limped into the surgery for his check-up and asked if I could call an ambulance. 'Why?' I asked. 'Well I just jumped down off the wall from the car park. I've broken my leg again but can you do the check-up quickly before the ambulance gets here?'

"We built a good relationship with the patients, many of whom were elderly and/or disabled, and I would often help them into the surgery from the waiting room myself, inevitably telling them to hurry up as I was a busy man. The patients themselves realised I wasn't being serious and loved it but the others in the waiting room were aghast, not realising that we knew each other well.

"I retired from dental practice in 2012. This gives us time to travel in our camper van, visiting lots of places in Britain to which we have never been.   I have watched England play cricket twice in Australia and in South Africa.   I also like gardening, playing golf and am still trying to become more proficient at the piano.   I have good days and bad days but enjoy the help that Roger Daniel, my former colleague, gives me.   Roger is well known, not only as an excellent musician but also for his dry sense of humour, and after one lesson had gone badly he asked me to do him a favour.   He said if ever I was asked to play the piano at his funeral it would be a kindness if I refused.

"I enjoyed my days as a practising dentist and was in favour of many of the changes that happened during my career.   However, recent increased regulation and rigorous compliance legislation took away the pleasure and increased the worry so I decided to retire in 2012.   Many people wonder why I didn't continue part-time but the fees for maintaining registration and professional indemnity insurance made it uneconomic which was a shame.   Dentistry has changed enormously during my 38 years.   Masks and gloves and cross- infection control procedures have become cornerstones of practice and use of white fillings and adhesive dentistry more common than old silver amalgam.   Expertise in making dentures has become a forgotten and undervalued skill.

"However, the most profound change I noticed was the transformation of children's teeth brought about by the introduction of fluoride toothpaste in the early 70s.   Anyone who did not have this in their early years, and they will now be in their 50s or above, will have many restored or extracted teeth, whereas the 40- year- olds and under now often have few or even no decayed or filled teeth.

"Prevention was really in its infancy when I started at dental school in 1967 but I feel that even today it is badly neglected by the dental profession.   I used to stress some basic rules for children.   Firstly parents should brush their teeth before bedtime until ten years old, and they shouldn't rinse out as the fluoride paste needs to stay in the mouth as long as possible.   And definitely avoid sweets and fizzy drinks before bedtime.   It is best to eat them all at once rather than over long periods.

Length of exposure is more damaging than the amount.

"I also used to teach that tooth brushing is not easy. To be effective one needs to concentrate and watch that all areas are reached by doing it in front of a mirror. The brushing for two minutes rule never made sense to me as I often demonstrated that I could cover everywhere in 40 seconds. Doing it for a set time just means moving the brush over the same easy places repeatedly and never reaching the difficult areas. And I fail to understand why everyone is told to floss. Most people, however well intentioned, can't do it properly so why do dentists continue to stress it? Far better to use spiral brushes which are easier to use and more effective. How I wish the dental profession would improve its quality of preventive advice and make it more realistic, practical and effective."

John's retirement is a loss to the profession. Few of us find a visit to the dentist pleasurable but one suspects a visit to John in practice was an exception.

Denise Pearson

What is it that gives individually owned shops an edge over most multiple shop branches in the community? Well of course they must satisfy a need uniquely well but above all they are friendly. Relating to customers in a sympathetic and listening way is the magnet that draws in the regulars. As people live longer many of them become lonely. They don't have much contact with other people but can find comfort where they are known by caring staff at local shops.

Fakenham still has a number of smaller shops which have not yet been squeezed out by multiple traders in the name of adapting to changing demand. Younger families have hectic, impatient lifestyles and the traditional atmosphere valued by older people is receding.

One highly valued local shop is Paper-Klip in Bridge Street. Its business is stationery, local books, computer cartridges, copying and photo service.

It has carved a professional niche in the town and further afield. But it also has Denise Pearson who serves the customers of all ages with calm efficiency, not least the old and lonely. Denise has been at Paper-Klip working with its owner Geoff Saunders for 20 years.

She says "Photo copying is one of our fastest growing features and as more customers – often at the urging of their IT numerate younger relations – become computer aware there is a growing demand for ink cartridges and other accessories. And older people still write letters. They correspond in hand writing and we supply a wide range of notepaper and envelopes. Hand written letters are far more telling of personality and more likely to be keepsakes than E mails.

"There is pressure on space as the business has grown. Our sister shop News-Klip which is now owned by Geoff's son Scott is also busy. We used to occupy part of it but expanded to the present site. The pressure on space is eased somewhat by the excellent service offered in obtaining supplies next day if an item is not available in the shop.

"My mother's family are from Great Massingham where I was born. I have one sister. We moved to Fakenham when I was five into William Road after my father built us a bungalow there. My father's roots were in Walsingham and he was in the building trade. I went to the local school in Queens Road and then onto the Grammar School but cannot claim to have been a top scholar. I went on to Kings Lynn Tech to do a secretarial course. I worked for Barnhams Electrical in Norwich Street for three years until 1985 when I left to have my first son. My marriage in 1984 to my first husband lasted for seven years until we divorced. We had two sons – Tom, who is now a postman and Liam, who is a media executive and now lives in Swindon. I met Lloyd my second husband 10 years ago and we were married in Cyprus this year. He is a maintenance engineer at Bespak in Kings Lynn. We moved back to Massingham this year are renovating a house there.

"When my children were small, from 1985, I helped out part time at the local playgroup in Fakenham until the youngest started school and I joined Paper-Klip.

"There used to be a busy general store in Weasenham Road, Massingham which my grandmother ran. Now there is one village shop and post office. The amenities in Massingham are limited but offer lots of clubs and entertainment to all ages and there is something for everyone. People who live in Fakenham generally have an affection for the town. Those who don't know it well may take a less favourable view but it certainly has hidden depths. There are interesting shops if you know where to look and our racecourse.

"The future holds challenges in that it is planned to build a further 800 houses just to the north of the town. What new job opportunities that will bring we do not know but it will put pressure on the amenities such as shops and services. The town was traditionally a centre for the printing industry and gas production but not any longer. If those new residents do not find work locally they will presumably look to Norwich or King's Lynn. However the population of Fakenham is likely to grow by several thousand and this should attract investment.

"If I have a regret it is that I did not try harder at school. My main skill is organising people and establishing routine. I keep calm and don't panic whatever the pressure. I believe I could have developed a broader outlook than Fakenham. As it is we have been lucky to holiday in many parts of the world. I loved the Dominican Republic, Antigua and the Gambia. Lloyd is a keen diver so we love Egypt. I also visited New York with a friend for her 50th and found it a very exciting city. I have a 12 year old dog called Archie who is a Cairn terrier cross. Now our next project is to finish off the garden by putting in some flower beds next year.

Drifters

This excellent fish and chip shop is one of the jewels in Fakenham's crown.   Owned and run by Jonathan and Mark Hollings and Andrew Felton, it occupies an iconic building in Oak Street. The business moved to this building fourteen years ago when the lease ran out at their previous shop behind the cinema. Mark has been with the business for 28 years, Jonathan for 24 years and Andrew for fifteen years.   The continuity and dedication shows in the quality product and service, which is their hallmark.   The magic of their success is that they are in tune with the local clientele, many of whom they count as their friends.   Mark and Andrew do the frying and Jonathan runs the 40-cover restaurant.   They have recently started a delivery service within a six- mile radius to the delight of many of their older customers and others.

"Jonathan explains: "It takes five minutes to fry fish and chips. Even when we are very busy, we limit our ready-fried portions to six and avoid the practice of many fish and chip shops of doing 40 or so ahead of their customers' arrival, and storing them for an undefined time in the hot cabinet. This can mean customers having to wait for their meal to be individually prepared for them but the benefit of quality satisfies most of them in an age where people are reluctant to wait for anything. Our menu contains a number of meat products with appropriate sauces and we have a special menu for the kids."

He continues: "Fish and chips, described by Winston Churchill in wartime when they were not rationed as 'the good companions', are still firmly rooted as a staple of British cuisine. Cod and haddock are plentiful but tend to be further afield than in years past. This is putting pressure on prices. Our fish is fresh caught and frozen immediately at sea. There are some unwelcome variations posing as more modern versions but connoisseurs of traditional fish and chips know the authentic dish when they see and more likely taste it. We use traditional batter, no beer batter for example, and fry in lard as fish and chips should be. The use of palm and vegetable oils does the dish no favours and anyway is coming under fire on health grounds. There is a dietary move towards gluten free and this puts batter, which contains flour, out of reach of those who pursue it."

Jonathan was trained and practised as a baker in his earlier career and is well equipped to present alternatives as necessary. He prepares desserts at Drifters, such as lumpy bumpy pie, and will make wedding and celebration cakes for friends and relations. Time permitting, and it seldom is, he loves craft baking, for example the traditional harvest wheatsheaf. Jonathan was married with two children and is now divorced. His son, who is a carer, has two children, a son and a daughter, the former is also a carer and his daughter, who has four children, has plenty to do looking after them. In total he has six grandchildren. And what does he think of Fakenham today?

"There are too many charity shops, estate agents and opticians. There is no men's clothes shop and no hardware shop. Shopping is my preferred hobby and I have to go from Fakenham to get many of the things I want. Dereham has a much fuller list of amenities, as does Holt. Somehow

Fakenham has been left out, but the planned increase in population brings the opportunity for new shops the town needs and we could also do with more parks.

"Drifters occupies a Graded II listed building in Oak Street which was previously the practice of John Plumber the dentist. Before that I believe it was a pub. There is an absence of employment in the town and the chocolate factory, the laundry and Aldiss rank as the bigger employers."

Jonathan and partner live at Wood Norton which has a scarecrow festival every other year. They have two dachshunds which need walks three times a day. For holidays Jonathan usually heads for his aunts and cousins who live in Las Vegas. "My luggage will include empty cases to fill up with purchases. I pack the empty cases into larger ones for the outward journey and fill them up for our return. It's not all casinos and gambling but we have our moments. For relaxation after work I like watching soaps on TV and particularly Downton Abbey and David Attenborough's wildlife programmes.

"We have had a number of celebrities visit Drifters. The Hairy Bikers were here, Roger Lloyd Pack and Rick Stein. Each year the staff of Drifters support a children's charity which sees us dressing up in costumes

...and chip shop in Fakenham, dressed up as characters from the musical Grease, are raising money for (front) Faye, Matt and Remy

Picture: IAN BURT

according to the theme. We have recently raised money to help two-year- old Remy Pope fly to the USA for urgent cutting- edge treatment for a brain tumour. (see Ian Burt's photo from the *Eastern Daily Press*). We have also supported the hospice at Hillington."

Fakenham Garden Centre

Brenda and Gordon Turner

Fakenham Garden Centre is the cherished feature of modern Fakenham created by the Turner family.

Gordon Turner, who comes from Suffolk, determined at an early age to make his career in horticulture and has accumulated an unrivalled experience over the last 50 years.

He says: "In 1963 I was working at the Barton Mills dahlia nursery in one of the coldest winters in living memory. I would cycle to work and then tackle my first job of the day, stoking the boilers which are essential to keep the plants in good order during the winter. I used to rake out the clinkers and, on one particular morning, the combination of the sub-zero temperature outside and the fierce heat of the boilers inside caused me the excruciating pain of frostbite on both ears. It took days to wear off.

"After a while, I moved on and went for a year to the Isle of Ely Horticultural College. After the course, students were expected to get some mud on their boots, so I worked at a vegetable farm in Surrey, growing salad crops with 30 other young people who had recently left college. Other members of the workforce came from Italy and Poland. Then I took a job in the fens with large- scale vegetable growers, Darby Bros, and this gave me my first management experience. I was in charge of the onion store, and the cold storage of celery, for huge customers such as Campbells Soups. I was there for three years and enhanced my horticultural knowledge immensely.

"It wasn't all work for I lodged at the Green Man pub at Methwold Hythe, which seemed to be open all hours and had an interesting landlady. Then I moved to Essex for three or four months to a vegetable farm bisected by the A12. This was a rough area, overlooked as it was by houses and flats.

"I was contacted by the vegetable farm in Surrey at which I had worked previously. They offered me an interview for assistant manager. I was 22 years old at the time. I got the job and was there for twenty years. After seven or eight years I was made manager of the 100 staff. There were 250 acres and we sought to grow three crops per acre per year. There was innovation too with a garden centre, a farm shop and 'pick your own' vegetables.

"One amusing story comes to mind concerning PYO. There was one couple of customers who seemed to spend forever in the broad bean and pea fields, and when they came to pay we discovered that they had shelled all the beans and peas and discarded the pods. We concluded this was no way to make money.

"I was interested in the possibilities of making a success of a garden centre for myself. Besides, there were a number of the owner's sons coming into the business, and I agreed with him that there would be no long- term role for me.

"I came to Fakenham in 1985. From selling our house in Surrey and moving into our new property, we lived in four houses in six months while I studied the opportunities for the small garden centre on the edge of the town. The printing industry which had been the heart of Fakenham had recently collapsed, and the town and community were going through a bad patch. However, new people were moving in, with higher expectations, and could be developed into a vibrant market. It was traditional that local folk grew sprouts and other vegetables in their front gardens, but this was not the ambition of the newcomers.

"The existing garden centre did not have assured quality suppliers and much of the stock was bought at random from Wisbech. There was a gap in the market and I decided to go for it. I bought the garden centre. In the first week I was warned that it would take 25 years to be accepted, and not to pull the wool over local eyes in the meantime. However, I never felt like a stranger for all that I was a 'blow in', and soon established good friendships with suppliers, customers and staff alike.

"The recession of the late 1980s made it difficult for trading, but we lived through that and growth resumed. Our main problem soon became lack of space to expand. The site itself is small, about 1.75 acres, and had been part of the old railway. The soil and its residue were difficult to upgrade, and we needed to condense our activities, adding value and

diversity as best we could. The garden centre needed to offer a wider range, working towards a one- stop shop for all our customers' horticultural and related needs. We introduced a landscaping service, initially on a 50/50 basis with the skilled contractor David Dyson, and when he retired after his wife's death, we took on the whole project. We also erected a covered area to give plants and customers protection from adverse weather. This enabled us to display a wider range of plants all the year round, and looked welcoming and attractive to our customers. We worked hard at coherent signage with plants in alphabetical sections so a customer knew where to look for roses, herbs, fruit trees, etc. This was particularly welcome in the outside displays. One cannot assume that customers have a sophisticated understanding of what they want and where to find it. Some have, but others appreciate useful information to enhance user friendly knowledge. The outside staff were on hand to help this process and give practical advice to those who needed it. We introduced garden furniture and clothes, and these features were much enhanced later on. Our pet care business has grown with the remarkable increase in consumer expenditure on pet care and accessories."

Through all these stages of Gordon's career he has been most ably supported by his wife Brenda.

She says: " In the early days I turned my hands to most things as required. We had a very small team to start with and the tasks had to be tackled. Everything from keeping the books to watering the plants, displaying the goods for sale and answering customers' questions, had to be done by the handful of us in the business. Today we have 57 staff .

She continues: "Our son Martin joined the business in 1997 and it really took off from 1998. He had gained a great deal of experience at horticultural college in Chelmsford and then with commercial companies, not least with the van Geest organisation. They had extensive vegetable farms in Lincolnshire, one of which was 1500 acres growing mainly cauliflowers and leeks."

On leaving Geest, Martin became assistant manager at Gordon's farm in Milford, Surrey where he had responsibility for rented farms growing vegetables in an area so extensive that he travelled 45,000 miles a year. He had 100 staff, with 60-70 in the pack house, but there was no future doing this for the rest of his career. So the search was on in the Turner family to find a separate garden centre for Martin to run. They found a possibility at Watton, but calculated that the cost and focus would be better channelled into Fakenham.

Martin takes up the story: "We had a café which was in need of development to realise its potential, and at the time was in the hands of a franchisee. We decided to take it in house. We had the good fortune to appoint as chef and manager Ross Watson, who was previously a chef at Sandringham, and his wife Kim, who is front of house manager. They, and the front of house supervisor, Carolyn Durrant, have made the coffee shop one of the main attractions of the garden centre, used by about a quarter of its customers.

Carolyn observes: "This is a high- quality destination and one of the leading attractions for our customers, who use it on a regular basis. We

see regulars for breakfast, others at lunchtime, and more in the afternoon. It is a venue in which women on their own or in couples can feel comfortable."

Carolyn is born and bred Norfolk and has established a rapport with countless customers not least those who are living alone, getting over the death of a partner or needing someone to relate to. She was brought up in Fakenham.

She says: "We lived in Hayes Lane until I was eleven. On leaving school in 1976, I went to work for a fortnight at the Mundesley holiday camp. I stayed six years but, as it operated only in the summer, I took a series of jobs out of season. These included working on the shop floor at Woolworths, and packing rations for Arab soldiers in McVitie's factory. Next I moved to Butlins, running bars for seven years. I gave birth to my little girl Nikki in 1987. I lived with my parents for four years and then went part time to Superbowl and became a full- time supervisor.

"I came to the Fakenham Garden Centre in 2006. There have been a lot of changes. Breakfast is a popular addition to our menu. We offer a range of homemade cakes and scones all day, and up to a dozen chef's specials on a menu which changes each week. We have baked potatoes, sandwiches and ham, egg and chips on every day, but such dishes as chicken, pea and bacon double crusted pie or lamb souvlaki alternate with other chef dishes so customers have something new or rotating every week. One of the most appreciated products is bread and butter pudding – my speciality - which was written up in the *Eastern Daily Press,* and scones, which are available every day to the delight of the customers. We have a takeaway service, and at special times such as Christmas, there is a masterclass feature."

Martin adds: "We are members of Choice Marketing a group of 33 garden centres, from whom we can source marketing leaflets and buy supplies. Their purchasing strength gives us an advantage which would not be possible buying alone.   They negotiate with suppliers, which removes another time- consuming burden. We designed our own logo and uniforms."

There has been a transformation of the layout and offerings in the shop. With the development of the new building for garden furniture and gifts has come a highly professional extension and layout of merchandise. The range of cards, calendars and books is augmented by interesting high- quality jams, chutneys, chocolates and confectionery.   It is also still possible to buy old- fashioned sweets such as acid drops, barley sugar or bullseyes in those old- fashioned tins that many other shops have long abandoned. The family touch is ever present. As from June this year Gordon and Brenda will have retired after 30 years of The Garden Centre.   Martin and his wife Jennie will carry on the business.

A recent innovation is serve yourself, loose frozen foods. This offers a new dimension for the single and elderly customers who want variety with choice but without waste.   The shop is transformed at Christmas time, and is a haven for children and their parents.   In January Martin and Jennie and members of the team visit the Christmas Show in Harrogate where they decide on the range for next Christmas.

Martin adds: "We have long been supportive of projects in the community. We supply over 80 Christmas trees for the festival in the Fakenham parish church, which has become nationally known. Visitors to the festival contribute money to the charities of their choice, and it is a major event in Fakenham. Every year we host the Fakenham horticultural show, and we support Save the Children. In 2015 the company received certificates in recognition of long term support. The masterclasses have been adventurous and well supported. This year we included one on Christmas nibbles which went very well. Most of them are Christmas related.

Further innovations are planned and there is more excitement ahead."

Willie Parker

William Parker's clockmaker's shop in Norwich Street was first occupied by the Parker family in 1890. At the time it was owned by the Aldiss family and the rent was £1 per week. Willie Parker's great- great- great-grandfather had moved their business from Walsingham, where they had been established since 1740, to Fakenham in 1840. Their first shop in the town was in Whitehorse Street, situated adjacent to the present day Conservative club. They can trace their family back to Wisbech in 1640. Norwich Street, Oak Street and the Market Place were the heart of shopping in the town. As late as 1932, when the population was about 3000, there were 24 shops and businesses in Norwich Street. They included two grocers, of which Home and Colonial was one, a butcher, greengrocer, two hairdressers, a fishing tackle shop, hardware, ladies' clothes, seeds and plants, a betting shop and other specialist outlets essential to the life of the town. There were also some twenty shops and businesses in Oak Street, including three butchers, a florist, the doctor's surgery, two dentists and a saddle and harness maker. The Market Place had another twenty shops and businesses, including five men's outfitters and clothing shops, International Stores, a piano and music shop and two chemists. *(Reference E M Bridges, Fakenham-Lancaster 2010).* Now Parker's is the only original shop left from that bustling period and gives one a flavour of how it must have been.

Willie had a job at a jewellers in London when his grandfather died, leaving his father to run the business singlehanded. Willie returned to Fakenham to help his father and went into partnership with him. He was a tough man who had been through the war and hard times. Like many of his generation, he did not worry a 'tinker's cuss' if he offended the people he did not like. This attitude extended to officialdom, and by the time Willie became a partner in the business there was some sorting out to do. Willie was given the cheque book and the accounts, and at the age of nineteen or twenty had to sort out the problems which had accumulated over the years. His enthusiasm for this sort of work was limited; nonetheless he coped with it.

Arthur Mason was one of those with whom Willie's father fell out. He explains: "He always wanted his own way, as some people do."

These were exacting times for the business, and it had to be adapted to its changing customer base. Willie Parker's father died aged 90 in 2005. By that time the printing trade had collapsed, with the sale of Cox & Wyman by its owners Thomas Tilling in 1982, and the business moved away from Fakenham. Other businesses such as Ross Foods and Jack Israel had closed and unemployment had reached 20%. It was a bad time and caused great disruption in the workforce. Willie's mother's brother, Uncle Fred Jude, who was managing director and a magistrate, saw it coming. He got out in 1980.

Jobs were found for some at Bernard Matthews and the chocolate factory, and small print- related businesses started up. While other towns, such as Holt and Burnham Market, were trading up to meet new consumer needs, Fakenham had long been an industrial town and fell behind when its main industry collapsed.

"Younger customers were inclined to shop on the internet, buying on-line and moving away from cash. At one time the business was primarily cash and considerable sums were involved. For example, there was the gamekeeper who spent £1000 in cash on a string of pearls at one visit. We had a big trade in selling sovereigns and other coins. While I undertook valuations for customers I did not buy from them or sell goods for them."

How?, I asked him, did he keep track of the valuables left for valuation and warranties in his busy and crowded shop when he had to cope alone? He replied that he was very careful. He added: "The skills base has shrunk in Fakenham. At one time there were five watch and clock repairers. Today there is just one in addition to me. I have many regular customers whose families have been with us for years and in some cases for generations. I have got to know their tastes and when something I think might interest them comes up I get in touch. For example, a pair of silver partridges was available recently and a beautiful silver snipe. I was able to put these in the way of a key customer.

There were a number of characters among them. Lenny Loose was a biologist and farmed mussels in Brancaster. He had a gardener who was a cross- dresser and was heard one day speaking to him on the phone saying he was wanted at a friend's house and make sure when he went he wore gardening trousers and not a skirt.

"We had an elderly lady customer talking to Father and she commented that she 'had seen the Light'. He looked up at the light in the shop and asked what was the matter with it. I had to kick his ankle and explain quietly that the customer had seen the Almighty.

"We had gypsies in the shop from time to time. They made and sold pegs, and might buy, but more likely steal, items from the counter. One such stole a ring and, wearing a long dress, tripped on the way out and sprawled on the floor. The ring was flung out and Dad picked it up. To her surprise, rather than call the police, he just told her to******off.

"One elderly ploughman accidentally ploughed his jacket into the soil. It contained his watch and both were buried out of sight. A year later he was ploughing again and uncovered his jacket. The watch was still in the pocket and in working order. The story got into the press who wrote that all Parker's watches could be relied upon to do that.

"At one time I had a number of properties as investments, but when my marriage ended in divorce I had to dispose of most of them. Now I have only a few left."

The marriage produced two sons but neither is interested in coming in to the business. One is a lobbyist in Brussels and has two children. The other is in financial services in Scotland and also has two children.

"There have been many changes in Fakenham and not all for the better," says Willie. "I don't like the development of endless fast- food shops. Potentially there are some good signs ahead with the prospect of a considerable increase of population in the town. There will need to be new amenities and new jobs to bring Fakenham into better balance and provide the work and quality of life to satisfy the new population.

"I still work six days a week from 8.00 a.m.to 4.00 p.m. and have had a heart pacemaker and hip replacement. I am less involved in Abbeyfield than I used to be. I have no regrets and still feel the pulse of the town. I have been very lucky in life."

Kathy Christianson

Kathy with Karen and Kathryn

Kathleen Stella Christianson is Norfolk born and bred. Her great, grandfather, Joseph Smalls, moved to North Creake from Southrepps, a widower with two small sons. One son, Joseph, became a basket maker in the village and married Rebecca Smith. They had seven children. Kathy's mother, Mary, was their second child.

"Joseph, my grandfather, had a thriving basket making business in North Creake that was known throughout Norfolk. He was a wonderful man and very knowledgeable. People came from all over for his advice on gardening, birds and basket making. He grew chrysanthemums and won many cups. He had the first penny- farthing bicycle in Creake and, at the age of 82 he cycled to King's Lynn and back one winter's day and nearly froze to death. He had to be lifted off the bicycle, given brandy and massaged to be restored to health.

My father, Charles Beales, came to North Creake to be taught basket making by Joseph Smalls and he married his daughter, Mary Smalls. They had six children of which I was the youngest, born in 1938. Charles Beales had a smallholding at the time but died of tuberculosis and his war wounds when I was just six years old. A favourite tale of my mother's was that if it was a moonlight night she would put me in the pram then walk to Creake abbey with my father. He would poach some pheasants he had spotted going to roost earlier and would hide them in the pram.

"When my mother was eleven, she had to take a test at school and as she passed this was able to leave school and go to work in a farmhouse at Holkham at one shilling a week. But it didn't last long as she was attacked by a horrid boy who lived there, who hit her across the back with a plank of wood. She gave him as good as she got and landed him a few good slaps. As a result she was told to leave and walked all the way home. Her parents insisted that she return to demand the shilling that was owed to her. Her granny had the shilling and bought a quarter pound of tea with sixpence of it.

"When my father died my mother was cook at the Althorpe Shooting Box in North Creake. The land girls lived there and my mother also worked on the land for a while. Mother received a small pension because Father had suffered shrapnel wounds in the First World War. The War Office wrote to her to ask how Father was, and she answered that he was still much the same as he had not deteriorated. In reply, they cut her pension by one shilling, which was a lot out of the ten shillings a week we had to live on. She was a lovely mother, living to be 98, a real country lady and we all adored her.

"The family was very poor. My brother Joe worked very hard as a teenager to provide food for us. The eldest four children had all already left home and joined various branches of the services, it being World War Two. I can remember tanks driving through Creake and soldiers marching. Planes would fly over Creake for ages in the evening and then again in the early morning. If they were low Mother would wake

Joe and me to come downstairs. Mum and Joe would be under the table and I went under the sink which, thinking about it, would have been sure death as it was a very large stone sink. One night we woke up to see a plane on fire crossing the village. It crashed in Granny's garden and both the pilot and navigator were killed. There is a memorial plaque to them at the gate of her house on Wells Road, North Creake, where the willows my grandfather used for his baskets also still thrive.

"It was a happy childhood, lived mainly outdoors, and it was considered a punishment if we had to stay in the house. I always had a cat. Two ladies called Gertie and Lotty lived near us and I remember them being very tall and always smartly dressed in velvet and high heels and it was those high heels which saved Gertie's life. One day she had rolled up a heavy rug which she threw out of the bedroom window for cleaning. It pulled her out of the window with it but her high heel caught under the bedstead and she hung there screaming until rescued. The two ladies always made a fuss of my cat until it left home to live with them. I was very upset but had a little revenge as my brother Joe bought a motorbike and on the day he started it up the cat was so terrified that it ran up their chimney, came down and ran all around the house covered in soot.

"I had TB as a child and at the age of eleven was sent to a sanatorium in Nayland, Essex. There was no education of any kind and no heating and the rooms for the patients, which had long sliding doors, were set on a veranda. The doors were only closed at night but otherwise left wide open whatever the weather, the only treatment at the time being fresh air. I have had snow blow across the bed and any liquid in the room would freeze in the winter. I was there for eighteen months, some of which was enjoyable. Other girls had been there for eight years and five years was about the norm. But the discovery of streptomycin changed all that. I was given it and went home after only eighteen months which was a record. Unfortunately, after another eighteen months my TB flared up again and I had another eighteen months in TB hospitals – initially at Kelling, which was very primitive, and then back to Essex. This time I had no visitors as the bus had stopped running. On my first stay in

Essex Mother had come every two weeks for two hours on a Sunday, that being all that was allowed for visiting. It was very hard on the young women with families as no children ever came.

"I remember that the village fete in North Creake used to be a big event as it was held for the war effort, usually in the vicarage garden. One year the Reverend Thornton, vicar of North Creake and a very tall man, squeezed his top half out of an upstairs window and rang a bell to make an announcement. He then found he could not get back in. The whole fete was transfixed, the children loving it. A ladder was brought and after much pushing and pulling he was hauled back in, to cheers. He was a real gentleman but it didn't stop him having a nickname. He was known as 'Froggy' but I can't imagine why. Almost everyone that was liked in the village had a nickname. There were 'Nobbs', 'Bubbles', 'Tin Tack', Gigolo', 'Shats', to name a few.

"My first job was as a telephonist at the airbase at RAF Sculthorpe five miles from home. I married an American service man and my life changed. I went to live in London first then Washington DC, back to London, then to Illinois, back to London, then to Arizona and from there to Turkey. In this time we had three children in three years – Gary, Karen and Steven-, and it was quite a struggle to move about with three small infants.

"In the late 1960s we had let our house in Northolt, London, and when we eventually returned to England to live we had a terrible time trying to get the tenants to vacate. Initially we all went to live with my mother in North Creake but then rented a house in Stiffkey. This house was clearly haunted and I was terrified the whole time. My son Gary felt the presence and would never be left alone in the house. When I went to bed I would often feel as if there was a strong breath blowing on my forehead and would wake in the night aware of a presence in the room which would not let me move or speak. Just before we left my daughter Karen was whisked down the back staircase. I was in a room close by and never heard a sound until she arrived at the bottom of the stairs. Karen was very upset and didn't know what had happened. I was never so happy to leave a house as that one. I have lived in 22 houses in my life and have never felt anything like that before or since. Strangely, after we had moved to Fakenham I met a man at a dance and told him that we had been living in Stiffkey. He asked me where and when I told him he said that his aunt had lived in that very house and nobody ever slept in the front bedroom as it was reputed to be haunted.

"We moved to Fakenham in 1970 and I have lived on Constitution Hill for 45 years. It has always been a nice little community. It is probably one of the steepest hills in Norfolk. Our house is called The Maples but on earlier deeds it was called Sunsct View and certainly when there is a fine sunset that house was aptly named. There have been some lovely characters living there. They include Mr and Mrs Tuck whose family had been bakers for many years. Mrs Tuck looked after all the old people who lived on the hill, making steam puddings and helping wherever she could. I remember one thing that I found funny at the time but she didn't. Mrs Tuck went to bed one night and woke up to find a mouse in her hairnet. They talked about that for a long time.

"One old couple on the Hill had a shoemender's business here and one can still find tacks and nails from his business in the gardens along with the stubs of slate pencils from the old infants' school at the top of the Hill. Ernie Grimes had a very successful market garden business at the top of the Hill in the 1970s/80s lots of people used to come up here to buy their plants. Ernie was engaged to Violet for 48 years but they never married.

"Two other local families lived well into their 90s. George Back, who lived next door, had been a Spitfire pilot and led a very interesting life. When he left, Ray and Evelyn Waters moved in. They were a lovely couple who had previously owned an antiques business in Wells. Ray as a boy lived on the Holkham estate where his father was a blacksmith. His mother died at an early age when he was quite young but he remembered her singing a lot as she had been on the stage. After she died his father had lots of problems, having been in the Great War. Ray

went to work on one of the estate farms and one day he fell off a stack and broke his leg. A man was coming by on his motorbike and picked Ray up and took him to Wells hospital. The man subsequently got to know Ray well and, realising how clever he was, paid for him to go to college. Ray flourished and held a very important job in the Second War co-ordinating all the farms in Leicestershire. So one might say Ray had a lucky accident. He died at the age of 96 and I miss him very much.

"For twenty years I worked in the Fakenham Ladybird Playgroup until some of the three- year- olds I knew and remembered grew up and brought in their own children. I felt I had seen the clock round and it was time to call it a day. During this period of my life I was divorced.

"Then I started a bed and breakfast business which kept me very busy for twelve years. I much enjoyed it and I met some interesting and diverse characters from many countries. The stories of this business would make a book in itself.

"I have been very fortunate to have as my neighbour Richard Powell. He is kind and helpful and an excellent photographer – he has produced the photos for this chapter and I have numerous others in colour.

"Growing and showing sweetpeas gives me great pleasure. I have entered them in local shows for many years and once at a national show in Bournemouth I won a prize. I also sell bunches of sweetpeas to Nigel in

Benbows, the Fakenham greengrocer in the Market Place.

"I am a member of the National Trust, the Forgotten Churches Society and the Fakenham and District Horticultural Association. I enjoy reading and going to the Fakenham cinema to see ballet and operas which are now transmitted there. My daughter and I like to go to exhibitions in London and we love the Chelsea Flower Show. I have a dear friend, Teresa Menday, with whom I visit houses, churches, art galleries and antique fairs. I feel very blessed with my family and friends.

"I am very proud of my children. Gary is a solicitor in Ludlow, Steven is a mental health therapist in Hellesdon, and Karen, who lives nearby and was once registrar in Fakenham, has raised a fine family. She makes amazing wedding cakes and has created a marvellous garden. I also have eight wonderful grandchildren.

"I have always liked Fakenham. There was a time when one seemed to know everyone and it was like a large village. But now people tend to keep themselves to themselves and it is harder to know so many people. Times have changed, mainly for the better because everything is comfortable and far less labour intensive".

Diana Braithwaite

Diana Braithwaite has demonstrated a high level of courage and determination in the face of many obstacles in her early life. She was born in Devonport in 1942, her father, a Quaker and a conscientious objector, was the target of consistent abuse because of his refusal to join the armed forces during the Second World War. After the war the family moved to Ealing in London and her father began a difficult search for work. Eventually he was employed as a personnel manager at the Hoover company in Perivale. The family moved to the first house of their own in Hanwell in the 1950s. In the next decade they moved to a new house in Shirley, Croydon, and her father was promoted to be a personnel director at Cheeseborough-Ponds. Five years later he died very suddenly of a heart attack at the age of 46.

At the age of eleven Diana contracted persistent appendicitis, then known as a 'grumbling appendix', which led to serious complications and four months in hospital. Her education was interrupted as there were no facilities for teaching in the hospital. She subsequently failed her eleven-plus twice and left school at seventeen for a pre-nursing course at the Chiswick polytechnic.

In her youth Diana was petite and disadvantaged by her health and interrupted education, but her experience in hospital made her determined to take up a nursing career and make a success of it – not least to show the pessimists what she was made of. Just in case she wasn't strong enough for nursing her mother persuaded her to do a secretarial course. However, this was not required as she gained a Part One SRN qualification at the age of eighteen and went into training at the Royal Free Hospital in London where she qualified as a staff nurse in charge of a children's ward. In 1964, she moved to the Mayday Hospital in Croydon. This was not a teaching hospital so the nurses had to cope with a wide range of medical complaints without the interventions of trainee or junior doctors. She started on a women's medical ward and then changed to casualty. She liked the work in casualty and soon after was made a junior sister.

At the same time a young doctor, John Braithwaite, had become medical registrar at the Croydon General Hospital two miles away. Diana and John saw progressively more of each other as the days passed and in 1968 they were married in Croydon Quaker meeting house. Since his undergraduate days at Cambridge John had wanted to be a GP in Norfolk. He had a close medical student friend at Cambridge in Sandy Greer, and at one time it was suggested that they should establish a practice together. However, that was not to be. At the time a doctor had to qualify in obstetrics and gynaecology in order to be a GP. John underwent this training at the Norfolk and Norwich Hospital where Diana became a staff nurse in the casualty department. When fully qualified John applied to join a GP practice in Fakenham. The partners could not have been more helpful. They rented a house for six months for the young couple during which the compatibility between them and the surgery could be assessed. This was successfully achieved as they got on well with their new colleagues.   John and Diana then bought a town house in Fakenham in which they lived for five years.

The nursing profession was very poorly paid at the time.   A nurse in training would be paid £11 per month plus board and lodging, while a secretary commanded a much higher salary and could always be sure of a job.   However, Diana pioneered the post of practice nurse at Fakenham surgery for six years without pay as it was government policy that GPs could not pay their wives.   This was seen as ridiculous hypocrisy as Members of Parliament were able to pay their wives up to £30,000 a year.   Fortunately the BMA eventually changed the rules and Diana continued working, with pay, for another twenty years.   In this work she would help the doctors by taking blood samples, undertaking ECGs for patients, running a diabetic clinic, giving 'flu inoculations and attending to patients' ailments within her level of training.

John was a dedicated Anglican so when they married at the Croydon Quaker meeting house the Quaker elders allowed the Bishop of Croydon to bless their union there.   However, they asked that he came wearing his black cassock only rather than his full bishop's regalia.   Eventually at the age of 35, Diana was baptised and confirmed in the Anglican Church so that she could take part in her husband's religious life.

In 1975 John and Diana bought the Manor House in the village of Shereford from the Raynham estate.   It is a large house and was in need of substantial repair but it has become a loved family home.   Much of the house is 200 years old and it is surrounded by a barn and other outbuildings, set in two and a half   acres of woodland and grass, alongside the upper reaches of the river Wensum.

John and Diana had two children.   The eldest is their daughter Amelia. She lives in Sussex with her husband Steve, a financial wizard, and they have a son and a daughter.   Amelia is just returning to nursing after being a full- time mother for the last seven years.   Their younger child Oliver now holds the rank of major in the army.   He has two sons and his wife Cathy has recently become deputy headmistress of Greshams preparatory school in Holt.

John and Diana were married for 26 years, but shortly after retirement John sadly died at the age of 60 from undiagnosed bowel cancer. He never had a scan as would be normal practice today. He was a fine man, well liked and respected as a doctor by his patients. He developed a hobby of glass engraving and became a guardian of the Anglican shrine at Walsingham. In subsequent years Diana became a volunteer steward at the Walsingham shrine out of respect of her husband's interest in the place.

During their early years, when John first arrived in Fakenham, they lived next door to a Mr and Mrs Bridges and met their son, Dr Mike Bridges. His profession was that of a soil scientist specialising in soil morphology, geography and land contamination. He lectured for many years at the University of Wales and eventually became Professor of Soils at an international institute in the Netherlands. Since his retirement he returned to Fakenham and has been active in Fakenham's Museum of Gas and Local History. Fifteen years ago Mike moved to live in Hempton and in the year 2000 Diana and Mike became partners. They live in a mutually supportive way in which Mike enjoys tending Diana's garden but Diana regards gardening as an extension of housework.

Diana's main hobby is choral singing. She sings in the Fakenham church choir, the King's Lynn Festival Chorus and the Thornhill Singers. The church choir sings occasional evensongs in Norwich and Peterborough cathedrals. King's Lynn Festival Chorus sings in local venues and has also been on tours in Belgium, Italy, Spain and Ireland. The Thornhill Singers are a group of friends who get together to sing on a Friday evening and take evensong and charity concerts to churches with no regular music.

Ashley "Sid" Wright

"My father serving in the British army was badly burned in the fighting in the Western Desert in 1942. When he recovered he was offered the choice of leaving the army or staying in and being posted to India. He chose the latter and I was born in Peshawar, then part of British India, August 1943.

"I had a wonderful childhood in India, a good education and so much diversity. I was sent to England in 1957 to finish my schooling and lived with various aunts and uncles in Burnham near Slough, and later in Hounslow, where I went to the secondary modern school. This was a poor exchange from the St Anthony's boarding school in Lahore in India where education standards were high and targeted on Cambridge entry.

"One of the family of relatives with whom I was lodged was a Jehovah's Witness. When I left school in August 1959 at the age of fifteen he asked me what I was going to do. I was crazy about aeroplanes and chose to join the RAF. This outraged him in that he thought my aim was to kill people, which it was not, and threw me out of the house with no provision for further family life and shelter.

"What was I to do?   No one was prepared to take a young man on, and eventually a friend, John Jones, lent me his tent in which I lived in the woods.   I took a job at International Stores in Datchet and later that year joined the RAF as a boy entrant in St Athen in Wales.   When I finished my initial training I was posted to RAF West Raynham.   It was a happy camp with camaraderie and I formed a lot of friendships.   There were fourteen of us to a room, we had to make our own entertainment, pay was low, we had little money but we looked after each other and shared what we had.

"My first visit to Fakenham was on a dank, cold, misty Sunday afternoon and I went to The Snack, a small café on Bridge Street where all the young people hung out.   'Blue Moon' by The Marcels was playing on the jukebox and, after all the places I had lived previously, I felt at last I had found a home and there was companionship.   I had nowhere to go at Christmas and a friend, Jack Wills, invited me to join him in Cornwall for the holidays.   I was bought a pint of scrumpy by Daphne du Maurier who was standing at the bar in the local pub.

"I spent four very happy years at West Raynham visiting various countries on detachments.   In 1961 I learned to fly at Raynham where I joined the Fenland Gliding Club and earned my pilot's licence flying tugs that launched gliders.   I still have and use it today at the age of 72.   In 1965 I was posted to Malta and later to Cyprus.   I had met Jane on 31st December 1964 at a New Year party.   I saw her for the first time singing on stage.   I determined Jane was the girl I was going to marry and our wedding was in August 1965.   She joined me in Malta where we made our first home together.   We returned to the UK in 1968, again to West Raynham, and then in 1970 to RAF Marham.

"I got the nickname 'Sid' whilst I was the youngest member of the RAF boxing team.   Another member, Doug Feeney, a Yorkshireman, referred to all as 'our kid'.   Another member of the team, Tony Breganza, made rhymes of everything so 'Sid the Kid' was born. Even my mother ended up calling me Sid.

"Our first son, Ashley, was born in Malta. Sadly he died aged 45 from motor neurone disease. We have two other sons: Gregory is an engineer and Bradley works for the local chocolate firm and is a part-time fireman. We have three grandchildren. From 1968 I served at Raynham and then Marham.

"I left the RAF in 1973 and joined the Cambridgeshire police. There were no vacancies in the Norfolk constabulary at the time but it was suggested that I try again at a later date. In the meantime I spent three very happy years in Cambridge city where there was excitement on every shift. I spent ten weeks at the Training School in Eynsham, Oxfordshire, and then my two-year probationary period commenced. I was aged 30 and sent for training to Parkside in the middle of Cambridge city.

"This was basic police work, for example, I had to check every door on my beat to ensure it was locked. Heaven help me if the sergeant found one unlocked on his spot checks. I had my first successes at that time. On checking one door in the dark a cat jumped out in alarm, a burglar fell out of a window above and I made my first arrest. He had been sought for multiple burglaries and CID had been looking for him for a while. Then I recognised a felon who had stolen Sir Vivian Fuchs' car and escaped from court. I recognised him from photos in the newspapers and gave chase. He ran into Clare College and after a search I found him hiding in the kitchen. He emerged looking for a chance to attack me. I hit him hard on the chin and put him in handcuffs."

"The population of Cambridge was 120,000 including a large number of students. I only made one civilian friend in Cambridge, Peter Harding, as a result of a macabre situation. I had to tell him that his father had died suddenly in Canada. His reply being proper English was 'You are a bit late, old boy, he died 32 years ago.' The message was intended for another Peter Harding but the control room had its wires crossed. When you work in a big city you do not have time to make friends as there are so many people to deal with.

"We had four panda cars, five or six foot patrols and a Black Maria. We used to meet up at a focal point at a derelict building which had a vending machine. On one occasion when we assembled, twelve dossers emerged from the building. We rounded them up and dropped them off on a road out of Cambridge at one mile intervals.

"I transferred to Norfolk Police in 1976 and we moved to Fakenham where Jane was born. We eventually bought the house we live in still. I served in Hunstanton from November 1976 where even the seagulls had moved out and I found it so boring after Cambridge city. I then asked for and was granted a transfer to Fakenham where I served from October 1977 until my retirement in May 1999."

Sid Wright had his own very effective methods dealing with felons. He served in the Norfolk Constabulary for 22 years of his 25 year police career and received 21Commendations. It was said there were two courts in Fakenham, one of them was Sid's court which was behind Woolworths. "All rules are made to be broken because most rules are rubbish. I tried to ensure that a villain would not offend again.

"My police career took off and on one occasion we nicked a gang who were accused of 147 house burglaries. We put them in cells far apart in the cell block so they had to shout to each other and this way we got all the information needed to book them. When it came to interview I said I did not need to ask them questions as I already had the answers.

"I had no interest in promotion. I was happy catching criminals and serving people. I already knew several people in Fakenham through Jane and formed a lot more wonderful friendships. My success as a policeman in Fakenham came because I treated everyone the same, from vicar to road sweeper, because I believed we all served the community in our own ways and everyone was as important as the next. I never talked down to law breakers or suspects but was resolute.   They knew I did not mess about   It is very significant that many of those I arrested and dealt with on the spot bore no resentment later in life and emerged as responsible citizens.   I would rather warn a petty criminal for a motor offence – faulty car lights for example - than book him.   They knew if I found them wanting again I would throw the book at them.   I gave many a silly law breaker a warning and a chance to mend his or her ways.   Lots of people I dealt with in Fakenham, whether as criminals or responsible for a minor offence, are now my good friends.

"This showed at my retirement party in May 1999 where there were enough people present to consume three hog roasts and whisky galore. A number of them were gatecrashers who heard we were having a party and wanted to 'wish me well!'

"Villages in Norfolk tend to be territorial with gangs forming.   I heard that there was going to be a riot in the Bridge Street car park and found it filling up with lads looking for trouble.   I told them that I was going away for ten minutes and if any of them were still there when I returned I would arrest them.   There were just five remaining and they were getting into their cars to leave.

"Guest speakers were invited to address groups of youngsters and on one occasion a famous movie star of Westerns was invited and plied with welcoming drinks before his speech.   He caught sight of my policeman's helmet and started hurling insults encouraging crowd disrespect.   I moved over to him and said I would not put up with disrespect to the Queen's uniform.   There was a horrified silence when I said "At one time I used to be like you but I overcame it." 'Oh yes,' he sneered, 'how did you do that?' I replied "I grew up." I was reported to my superiors who had been told I had brought a visitor into disrepute. I said I was not going to have the Queen's uniform insulted by anyone and if they took a different view I was obviously in the wrong profession.

"My favourite watering hole in Fakenham was the Conservative Club where I made many friends. There were characters such as David Topping, Derek Smith, Bushy, Stylo and Jim, now sadly departed but not forgotten. One who thankfully is still with us is Paul Ramm. On one of my visits to the club, drinks were flowing quicker than Niagara Falls and I asked Derek, the landlord, what was the occasion. He replied that it was his birthday. Stupidly I said, 'Its mine tomorrow.' Derek told me to make sure I got down to the club tomorrow and we'd have another party. I felt 'obliged'. On this day I made sure I did not have much to drink as I was working a twelve –hour shift at Holkham Hall the next day (a much sought-after duty).

"On my way home that evening, and sober, I tripped on the kerb at the traffic lights and to avoid falling face first into the rose bushes I twisted and fell, breaking my ankle. I dragged myself to a bench and sat there in agony wondering what to do. This was before mobile phones. I decided to crawl home on my hands and knees and started along the pavement where the small stones felt like boulders. I crawled on the pavement for what seemed like months, several cars passed , the drivers thinking, 'Sid's pissed again', (When they found out later the true position they felt bad). When I reached the grass verge I thought it would heaven be to crawl on but then reality hit me that this is where the dogs poop so back to the pavement and it felt like another six months. I eventually got on to my drive and by then my foot was so swollen I removed my shoe and went indoors. Down comes Jane: 'Where the hell have you been and where is your shoe?' 'I've broken my ankle and my shoe is outside,' the terror of Fakenham police replied. 'Get out there and find it' and the hero because he had found his match, crawled out and returned with the shoe to keep the peace.

"Many people say it must be easy to police Fakenham after a city like Cambridge. I found it harder and more personal because many of the incidents I dealt with, from fatal car accidents to cot deaths, burglaries and drownings, I knew the people and the family and became personally involved. An example was on 31st May 1981when I dealt with a triple fatality when three teenagers were killed. I was speaking to one of them twenty minutes earlier when his car broke down. Now I was dealing with carnage and his dead body. The other two teenagers I also knew and their parents too. This affected me personally very badly. The fourth teenager, a young lady, was critically injured but thankfully survived. I am now good friends with her and her parents.

"I finished duty that day at 5.00 a.m and was back on duty at 7.00 a.m. the same day. By 7.15 a.m. I had my first call and was dealing with a friend who had shot herself in the stomach in a suicide attempt. I am glad to say she survived. In Cambridge city people were statistics. In Fakenham and around they are friends.

"When the police helicopters were commissioned they brought a new crackdown on armed robbers, joyriders and other high- speed car crime. Road car chases at high speed can cause accidents and get more dangerous as traffic grows on the roads. But a helicopter flying at 1000 ft gives a bird's eye view and denies hiding places in remote countryside. Many times suspects are unaware that they are being tracked until a signal from the air to ground patrol intercepts them." Sid was one of three officers to be air observers.

Among the 21 awards and commendations Sid received during his 25 years in the police force was an International Award for Bravery. "I believe with one other officer PC Paul Stearman we were the first policemen in the UK to be awarded certificates under the GiancarloTofi Award Scheme, which are made annually to a member of any of the emergency services in his memory, following his death in 1972 while attempting to rescue a victim of a road accident. There have been just thirteen awarded worldwide since it was instituted.

"Our award followed the deliberations of a panel in Italy following an incident in June 1992 in North Norfolk. As reported in the Press at the time:

"The two officers were called to a road accident involving a car and a lorry on the outskirts of Fakenham. The car driver was trapped in wreckage under the lorry when flames began to burst around him. The two officers tackled the flames at close range with fire extinguishers. Despite their efforts the vehicle exploded and they were forced to withdraw. The two officers put themselves in real danger in an attempt to deal with the fire and rescue others."

"There are some funny sides to a policeman's lot, in reflection although not at the time. On one occasion I and two colleagues, PCs Alan Newton and Mick Irwin, had to accompany the bailiffs to Hindolveston to evict a smallholder who had not paid his bills. On entry to his house with the others I was confronted with what I thought at the time was the biggest pig I had ever seen. It was interested only in me for some reason and with its head down started to chase me at speed. Two things in sport at which I was absolutely useless were long-distance running and the high jump. On that occasion I reckon I broke the world records for both and I believe I hold them still. My escape was made by climbing a tree with the pig looking up at me and the others in hysterics."

In 1994 Sid marched in the Remembrance Sunday parade at the Cenotaph in London representing the Norfolk Constabulary. He retired from the police force at the early age of 55 in 1999 after more than 25 years service. It was a reflection of the strange pension rules. If he had stayed longer, and many tried to persuade him to do so, he would have lost a significant amount of pension.

"I stood for the town council and won my seat with 583 votes which was more than 400 ahead of my nearest rival. In retirement I spend my time enjoying my family, my grandchildren, my allotment, my vintage 1949 Riley which I spent eighteen years restoring, and I rebuild vintage lawnmowers and rotovators, and build and restore model steam traction engines, some of which are 105 years old. I have a workshop where I renovate anything with a motor and I have restored an airplane. I also fly aeroplanes, am a qualified instructor and teach people to fly gliders. "Jane keeps busy, does a little cleaning job and keeps me and the family in order.

"We value good relationships with the community and I would like to say a thank you to the people of Fakenham for being my friends and giving me a happy home."

Tim Aldiss

"I went to Gresham's School where, to my regret, I did not work very hard.   I preferred history and art to most other subjects but my star memory is geography as taught by the excellent Dick Bagnell-Oakley. I can still remember much of what he taught me. What he put into my ear tended to stay there whilst in other subjects taught by less effective teachers much of what entered one ear went straight out of the other one. Not only was he good at his subject but he could be interestingly diverted, for example I can remember learning all about cuckoo spit from him. He was well known in Norfolk for he used to read the news on *Look East.* The art master was Stewart Webster who was a Fellow of the Royal Institute of Water Colours and who inspired his pupils to use their talents.

"From an early age I was pushchaired around by the river at Goggs mill by Jean Rose and learned to fish for tiddlers. But aged eight or nine I had my first experience of fly fishing, inspired by Fred Parker who lived in Westmead Road. He also inspired my father to fish and this made a strong father- and- son bond between us. I had met Fred Parker on the riverbank. He was marvellous with children although he and his wife Ethel had none of their own. He also taught me to shoot an air rifle and play chess and drafts.

"My brother Bill, who was four years older than me, had a keen interest in horses and was active in the pony club. I walked in his footsteps, as brothers do, and learned to ride. This gave me another lifelong interest.

"It was not expected that I would automatically enter the family business. My father, who was a thoughtful man, offered me a choice of career, but I am sure he hoped that I would go into the family business. I had a hankering to be a farmer. My vision of it was that I should be a farm labourer for a year or two, go on to farming college, and then my father would set me up on a 1000- acre farm where I would spend an idyllic life. My father supported my working as a farm labourer but made no commitment as to future broad acres. He was a wise and wonderful man, and if I had lived my life half as well as he I would feel that it would have been even more worthwhile.

"It did not take me long to adjust to reality. The farm labourers with whom I worked regarded me as a posh, public school boy, and gave me all the most unpleasant jobs to do, following long tradition. These included clearing the trash that clogged up under the thrashing elevator so the lads could continue their work. There was all- pervading dust it was impossible to escape. Then there was 'knocking up', which meant separating the clods of manure thrown up by the muck spreader in the fields. It was soul destroying. If I stuck with it as the start of a farming career, without any guarantee that I would get a 1000- acre farm at the end of it, I might well end up on a council farm of 50 acres which did not match my original vision at all.

"I stuck it for eight months - and my father suggested I take a gap as a reward. He gave me £60 and I set off by land and sea to visit Ibiza. It was the only way to get to it at the time, and there was nothing there, other than two hotels, when I arrived. However, it opened my eyes to travel and new experience. When I returned, I went straight into the shop which was my real chosen career.

"On my first day I was shown how to dust and sweep the wooden floors by scattering and sweeping up 'Dustmo' which cleaned and disinfected the surface. I was also told by my father that I could not call him Dad in the store. Then I went away on courses to manufacturers, which included blankets in Witney, linen in Northern Ireland, and sheets and towels in Lancashire, to see how they were made, all of which was good background for working in a drapery store.

"I loved it from the beginning, and went through all aspects of the store – fabrics, linens, materials, haberdashery, retail furniture, ladies' fashions and on buying expeditions. At the end of this training, I could claim to have done every job I would ask others to do.

"My father was one of seven, and the Aldiss family owned a large amount of property in Fakenham, until the Aldiss estate was dissolved in 1968/9 when most of the properties were sold for a total of £128,000. This included the Home and Colonial grocery shop in Norwich Street which had been bought in 1932 and leased out to H&C on a 30- year lease with no rent rise. The great depression, in the early 30s, made it very difficult for landlords who wanted solid anchor tenants, hence the 30 year lease. The properties were sold because some of the family were worried they had too much exposure to it, with the prospect of swingeing death duties. It was good time to sell. Nobody foresaw the horrendous inflation that was coming. The estate was managed for years by auctioneers, Long & Beck and then Percy Howes before it was sold to the Grainger Trust. My mother was sensible and practical and persuaded my father that we should own the premises from which we traded. This meant they had to buy back these premises from the family, but it proved to be good advice.

"Father was a committed church goer, a churchwarden and district councillor. He raced Norton motor bikes as a young man. Mother was born in London in 1914 and grew up in Raynham. She sought security throughout her life. In the early 1930s she spent three years as companion to an impoverished aristocratic lady in Brussels, and showed her, among other things, how to turn worn cuffs and make do and mend. While she was in Brussels my father wrote to her every day and she kept all his letters. She instructed that they should be burned when she died. I had this task to do, and it took me months to action it. Though I never read any of the letters, they were nonetheless a link between my parents and the thought of burning them was distasteful. However, in the end I carried out my mother's wishes.

"My parents were married in 1934. In 1922 my grandfather had bought a holiday beach house on Scolt Head off Burnham Overy Staithe. Romantic as this might have seemed to me as a child, it was in fact a converted railway carriage, as many of them were. My holidays consisted of ponies and fishing and boats which made for an idyllic childhood. Years later, in 1946/7, I helped Billy Haines pull down the huts and, in so doing, lost a biro - a very expensive and rare writing instrument at the time, and which had been a present from my father. I remember such characters as Miss Disney, who seemed to be impervious to the cold, dressed very casually in a gym slip. She was a teacher.

"While my father sailed in the variety of boats my family owned, I preferred the motor boat *Wheezyanna,* which we later sold. My family tried to buy it back as a 70th birthday present for me but it was not available.

"Through the 50s, 60s and 70s the business thrived and expanded. In 1988 we decided to move the Aldiss furniture store, which occupied 17000 sq. ft. on two floors in Norwich Street. This had the disadvantage that the staff employed on the ground floor had to go up to the first floor when a customer wanted service there. This meant that there was a depleted number of staff on the ground floor sometimes when we needed them all there. It became difficult to trade from it so we searched for much larger premises, and on my 50th birthday we moved it to part of the old Fakenham press and printing works, which gave us almost unlimited scope. The business thrived and still does, and is a major player in the county.

"We had considerable help from the North Norfolk District Council who always had Fakenham's interests at heart. It had been a difficult period. The printing industry had been sold out, Ross Foods were consolidating and Jack Israel onions, on what is now Jewsons site, had closed. Furthermore the closure of Raynham and Sculthorpe had contributed to unemployment reaching 20%.

"Fakenham is a wonderful place, the gateway to North Norfolk. It has everything going for it, a lovely Georgian centre and a beautiful church. It also has great facilities, the racecourse, the golf course, sports centre and the river Wensum. There is a thriving industrial base, largely in building and engineering and a number of print and design businesses. One recent success, on a much larger scale, is the chocolate factory and another is the former Stella McCartney frozen food factory, now owned by the big American food corporation Hains Daniel. The town boasts most of the major supermarkets as well as independents, like my company, the Fakenham Garden Centre, Langham Glass and Pensthorpe to name a few, and we are earmarked for huge expansion with the prospect of 900 new homes. I would say the future looks bright.

"Penny and I married in 1964. Our marriage lasted for 41 years until we divorced. We have two daughters: Charlotte, now 49, sailed across the Atlantic with a crew of ten in 2015 and Arabella, now 47, with two beautiful children, Jake and Tate, who is married to American Eric Kump, skilled in private equity, who has helped us a great deal in the business. Penny has been a director of the business for many years. Now, at 77 years of age, I have moved from day- to- day management of the business to be chairman. It is a role I much enjoy, supported as I am by some really excellent executives. The managing director now is Paul Clifford, who joined us after a distinguished career in the trade. He has all the things a modern business needs to make the right decisions. When he was appointed his dedication was such that he drove every day for years from London to Fakenham and back.

"Domestically I have a new partner.

"Aldiss has long had a policy of giving people a good deal. There is a saying in the trade that 'turnover is vanity and profit is sanity'. But we have proved, time and again that, if our turnover is high enough, we qualify for better discounts and prices from our suppliers, so we can achieve both. Some of our competitors disapprove of our focus on turnover, but no doubt they have their reasons.

"In my less hands-on role, I can pursue my favourite occupation which is fishing. I have developed this interest, which has taken me all over the world. All the fish I catch abroad is returned to the water, so I use barbless hooks and take great care not to handle the fish unnecessarily. I use flies wherever I fish, and it requires skill and patience with, for example, milkfish in the Indian Ocean, which swim with mouth open, ingesting plankton.   The skill is to place the fly in the path of one of them so it sucks it into its mouth.   It can take days to achieve this, and over an hour to land one, once hooked.   I also catch bone fish which one cannot eat.   I return the catch to the water so this is not an issue.

"International fly fishing has an interesting community of enthusiasts, and whether I am in Russia, Argentina, Alaska or the Seychelles I am likely to meet fellow fishermen.   I have a considerable collection of antique fishing tackle, which is growing.

"I started game shooting at the age of 68 and gave up hunting some years ago.   I also comb the beach for stones which can be polished, and this has resulted in a fine collection suitable for necklaces or costume jewelry.   It is amazing what one can find on the beach.   The stones include carnelians and agates, and the possibility of a piece of amber.

"I have been fortunate in life.   I love Fakenham and it has been very good to me and my family.   I was born with a silver spoon which I am extremely reluctant to throw away.   Perhaps if I had done so I would have taken more risks.   But who knows…?"

Pensthorpe – Bill and Debs Jordan

Pensthorpe Natural Park was founded in 1988 by Bill Makins, to encourage the breeding of a wide range of exotic waterfowl. He knew Peter Scott well and was inspired by his work and imagination. Gravel extraction on the 700-acre site was carried out in the 1970s, and the subsequent work was to restore the areas with sensitivity, leaving lakes with gently sloping banks, allowing marginal plants to establish with their associated invertebrate life, providing a food source for waterfowl.

Debs Jordan, who had been born and bred in Ringstead, Norfolk, was the daughter of farmer David Pull. She met Bill Makins by chance on a day trip to Pensthorpe with her two children aged five and seven at the time. The children spent the day collecting the moulted feathers from around the reserve which when she met Bill Makins that day she assured him had been gathered from the ground rather than plucked from any living birds. She was enchanted by the unique atmosphere of the park. "It was a near spiritual experience," says Debs, who communicated her enthusiasm to Bill Makins. He was in the process of selling Pensthorpe but the negotiations had fallen through twice at the last moment. Debs' husband Bill Jordan's family had been millers in Bedfordshire for 150 years. In 1960 they introduced a 'granola' toasted cereal after a visit to California. Their timing was very much in line with the change in eating habits. This was down to a number of factors, including growing awareness of health issues and the benefits of a balanced diet. Wholegrain cereals and fibre were particularly important, rather than over-processed equivalents. Oats, primarily, were highlighted as having real functional benefits due to soluble fibre which helps reduce cholesterol. In the 1970s Jordan's launched their Original Crunchy range of cereals, flours which were near 100per cent wholewheat, and mueslis, which were all packed in biodegradable materials. The cereal market was moving from more traditional cornflakes eaten at the table alongside bacon and eggs on the menu to 'breakfast on the move'. This movement inspired the Original Crunchy bar.

Jordans' innovations stretched far beyond cereals. Jordans took a giant leap into the field of sustainability, directly influencing their supply chain by buying only from 'Conservation Grade' accredited farmers. This farming practice centres around wildlife, neither intensive nor organic, and proves that the firm's beliefs ran far deeper than just healthy eating, with consumers buying a product from a healthy landscape.

Bill formed the Guild of Conservation Food Producers, whereby farmers, contracted to grow cereals to Jordans' specifications, signed up to dedicating ten per cent of their acreage to sustainable support for the natural environment and its wild animals. Environmentalists and scientists come together to design farm management protocols, which eventually saw 20,000 tonnes of grain and oats per annum being supplied to Jordans for their use in their breakfast cereals.

Bill, and his brother David, grew this fast- moving business to the point where they realised it was becoming too big for the two of them to manage and achieve its true potential. They both made the hard decision to sell the family firm, in 2007, to Associated British Foods, a far larger company that would be able to continue to grow and develop the Jordans brand.

The possibility of buying Pensthorpe Natural Park fitted with Debs' and Bill's vision spectacularly and the deal was signed in 2003. With this deal, they inherited a large exotic waterfowl collection; however, their real passion is focussed more towards native species conservation. So Bill Makins introduced the Jordans to Tim Nevard, a leading conservation expert, who helped with the formation of Pensthorpe Conservation Trust (PCT), a charitable trust that has developed the work of its predecessor, Pensthorpe Waterfowl Trust.

The PCT is dedicated to the conservation of wetland and farmland bird species through captive breeding programmes in national conservation partnerships. They are partners in three such projects: The Great Crane Project; the Corncrake Reintroduction Project, and Operation Turtle Dove and, working with David Stapleford, the leading expert in breeding captive red squirrels, the Trust acts as the hub for the East Anglian Red Squirrel Group which has seen kittens released on the Isle of Anglesey.

Bill says: "We have been involved with the ten-year Great Crane Project from the beginning and visited Wisconsin in the USA to learn how reintroductions were carried out at the International Crane Foundation. We also talked with the RSPB and Wildfowl and Wetlands Trust about restoring cranes to the UK, and so the project was formed. At one time cranes were widespread in Britain and much of this is commemorated by towns and villages with 'CRAN...' in their names. For example, Cranbrook and Cranley, etc. It was a shame for us that the release project was taken to the south west, however cranes travel long distances so I'm sure we will see released project birds here in the Wensum Valley soon."

Debs continues: "Chrissie Kelley is head of species management and is responsible for our release programmes ensuring that the areas designated follow the guidelines of the International Union for Conservation of Nature. Chrissie says: "This makes people think through the project and its feasibility. We need to consider the impact on the wild population. Breeding for aviculture is very different to breeding for release and we need to be sure that any birds released into the wild stand the best possible chance of survival. We have released 100 birds from Pensthorpe into the washes, and at present we are trying to breed turtle doves for release. They are seriously endangered."

"One of our major objectives," Debs says: " Is to encourage young people to take an interest in wildlife and conservation. There has been waning interest among the young who spend less and less time outdoors and are often constrained by their parents to stay 'safe indoors' and entertain themselves with internet accessories. Lack of exercise and fewer chances to explore their outdoor surroundings are part of the reason for widespread obesity, and for many of the anxiety problems from which the young and their parents suffer today.

"We seek to interest them with the history of Pensthorpe, which is recorded in the Domesday Book, and goes back for millennia before that, as witnessed by the finds of a mammoth tusk, axe heads and other features which can be seen on our Wensum discovery tours. These set out three times a day in the summer, using our 28-person coach. Pensthorpe was bigger than Fakenham in the middle ages and has been designated a Special Area of Conservation centred on the river Wensum which is a chalk stream. It is also designated a Site of Special Scientific Interest (SSSI). We have sulphur trails, spider and bug walks and pond dipping.

"There is a vibrant young team working at Pensthorpe, whose aim is to involve more families in Wild Rootz, the outdoor play area through nature education with play and fun. This, with its winding stream and man-made hills allow children to crawl through tunnels in educational play. Fact circles are posted around the area which offer both parents and children 'sound bites' of interesting information for them to take away with them. There are opportunities to 'meet the hedgehog' and 'meet the owl' on their journeys of discovery. The children are led around the lakes and woods with the use of a passport, packed full of activities, including the bug walk and stamper trail, to engage with families and more closely link them in with the wider reserve. It is an ever evolving project ."

"The outdoor facilities are weather dependent, and we have recently completed the transformation of Hoots House indoor play, which is sympathetic with the outside environment in that it is all wood fitted. This new facility means that Pensthorpe is a year round attraction whatever the weather."

The estate's luck changed when it had a visit from wildlife presenter Bill Oddie. He had come to film Pensthorpe's corncrakes for his television series The Really Wild Show and, whilst he was there, Debs took the opportunity to ask him for a photo. She recalls: "He not only agreed, but said that we could put whatever caption we wished on it. Some six months later we were approached by the BBC *Springwatch* television programme, which was looking for a new venue after filming for three years in Devon. Unbeknownst to all of us, Bill Oddie had put Pensthorpe forward for consideration because of its diversified wildlife and range of habitats. It changed our fortunes.

"The team, consisting of 100 cameramen, technicians and support staff, returned for three years to capture Pensthorpe's vivid wildlife on film. Their equipment cluded 25 miles of optical cable, connecting 50 cameras which could be operated by remote control. This not only monitored progress at each location but minimised the disturbance to wildlife. The programme had something for everyone, for example, nesting boxes could be erected in gardens and near school buildings , with appropriate feeding programmes for birds and insects. Also, how to encourage hedgehogs to live and hibernate. It opened up interest in the outdoors. We were delighted that the program catapulted not only Fakenham but also Pensthorpe on to a national stage.

More recent developments reflect Debs' and Bill's sympathy for and desire to recognise and make tolerable health conditions which can undermine the quality of human life, and that are suffered by growing numbers affected by loneliness, anxiety and insecurity. Pensthorpe is a spiritual place, offering something different and having the power to help you feel better. In their building refurbishment programme they have converted the former *Springwatch* studio, a listed building made up of five workers' cottages, into seven studios designed as consulting rooms, five of which have been let to Creative Chiropractic, with the remaining two for alternative treatments. There is a strong emphasis on 'mindfulness', notably for young people who are struggling to handle their emotions in today's hugely competitive and tough environment. Soon yoga and pilates classes will be offered from a new function/garden room. This room will be able to host receptions, parties, talks and training and will lead on to a private water garden of tranquillity and calm.

There are plans to buy Pensthorpe Hall, the large house situated overlooking the drive into the Natural Park, and convert it for the enjoyment of visitors to the reserve as overnight accommodation.

As Debs puts it: "We want to create Pensthorpe as a unique and incredibly important site, not just as a nature reserve. We want to re-create the Pensthorpe Village."

She and Bill have a most impressive track record of seeing and realising opportunity. This is all good news for Fakenham where the Pensthorpe experience has great potential to be a unique destination in the future of the town.